Praise for
Building Student Resilience, K–8

"Resiliency is a key to the intellectual and emotional development of students. Unfortunately, too many educational policies focus on threats and punishments rather than resiliency. Gabe Simon's splendid book is a welcome antidote for teachers and administrators who want to improve student results, but who also love and care for the students they serve. With an astonishing amount of evidence from a wide variety of sources, Simon makes the definitive case for strategies that are practical and effective. Best of all, Simon amplifies the power of his evidence through the voices of students. The reader is compelled to engage in what the author calls "tenacious caring" not because it raises test scores, but because it is the moral imperative of our profession."

—Douglas Reeves
Founder, The Leadership and Learning Center
Author of *Leading Change in Your School*

"Virtually all educators endorse the general idea that students will be more successful in and connected to their schools if they have the benefit of caring relationships and high levels of engagement. The challenge, of course, is determining how schools can create these conditions for every student. *Building Student Resilience, K–8* provides the answer to that challenge. It offers specific steps and tools educators can utilize in their schools and classrooms. Furthermore, it offers a novel idea for assessing the levels of caring relationships and student engagement in a school— asking the students themselves. This book has a lot to offer. I recommend it highly."

—Dr. Richard DuFour
Educational author and consultant

"Dr. Simon starts this book with a reminder from the late, great, Dr. Ron Edmonds that schools can still override almost anything happening in the life of a child. With the use of basketball and sports analogies, inspirational quotes, templates for student success, and detailed analysis of data, Dr. Simon provides concrete strategies for propelling 'at-risk' youth. In using scientific methodology on student risk behaviors, student resiliency, teacher practices and student test scores to show what school teams and especially school leaders can accomplish in obtaining improved student outcomes, Dr. Simon makes certain his readers will get results. GAME ON!"

—Dr. Crystal A. Kuykendall

Author of *From Rage to Hope*

"This is a wonderful, well-researched book, full of statistics and practical strategies that work for at-risk youths and those from high-poverty environments. It is a must-read for any practitioner working with these students."

—Ruby Payne, PhD

Author of *A Framework for Understanding Poverty* and
From Understanding Poverty to Developing Human Capacity

"Most learning starts from 'not knowing' or making errors. Resiliency, therefore, is among the most critical factors in helping students try again, engage in deliberate practice, and develop a fundamental skill of learning. Gabe Simon's book is the right mix of theory and practice that demands a call to action to create turning points for all students by developing their resilience in the face of risks. A must read, particularly for school leaders, as it shows that developing resilience is key to then raising achievement in a school."

—John Hattie

Author of *Visible Learning*
Director, Melbourne Education Research Institute

"An excellent resource for planning for today's schools. Make your school a caring community for all students!"

—Pamela B. Maxwell

Principal, Peace River School District

"This book offers excellent resources to support the social and emotional needs of students. The current emphasis on achievement scores has focused on the academic development of our students, but this book provides the resources needed to support the whole child."

—Edward C. Nolan

Supervisor of Mathematics, PreK–Grade 12
Montgomery County Public Schools

BUILDING

Student
RESILIENCE
Strategies to Overcome Risk and Adversity
K–8

Gabe Simon

CORWIN
A SAGE Company

CORWIN
A SAGE Company

FOR INFORMATION:

Corwin

A SAGE Company

2455 Teller Road

Thousand Oaks, California 91320

(800) 233-9936

www.corwin.com

SAGE Publications Ltd.

1 Oliver's Yard

55 City Road

London, EC1Y 1SP

United Kingdom

SAGE Publications India Pvt. Ltd.

B 1/I 1 Mohan Cooperative Industrial Area

Mathura Road, New Delhi 110 044

India

SAGE Publications Asia-Pacific Pte. Ltd.

3 Church Street

#10–04 Samsung Hub

Singapore 049483

Acquisitions Editor: Jessica Allan

Associate Editor: Julie Nemer

Editorial Assistant: Lisa Whitney

Project Editor: Amy Schroller

Copy Editor: Deanna Noga

Typesetter: Hurix Systems Pvt. Ltd.

Proofreader: Joyce Li

Indexer: Judy Hunt

Cover Designer: Cristina Kubota

Permissions Editor: Karen Ehrmann

This book is printed on acid-free paper.

MIX
Paper from
responsible sources
FSC® C014174
FSC
www.fsc.org

12 13 14 15 16 10 9 8 7 6 5 4 3 2 1

Contents

Preface   vii

About the Author   ix

Introduction: Turning Points   1

    Our Current Landscape   2

    Rebounds: Resiliency Overview   5

    The Need for Turning Points   7

    Including Student Voices in the Game Plan   9

    The Significance of This Work   9

1. How Do We Know They Will Bounce Back?   11

    Evidence From the Record Books   11

    The Impact of the Resiliency Protective Factors   13

    Summary of Theoretical Base   14

    Seminal Work on Resilience: The Kauai Study   16

    Specific Resiliency Protective Factors Impacting
Student Achievement   17

    Conclusion   24

2. The Caring School Team   25

    The Schoolwide Game Plan   25

    Students' Perspectives on Support   25

3. The Engaging Classroom Team: The Classroom Game Plan   39

    Perspectives on Engagement   39

    Practical Applications   42

4. **What We Urgently Stand For and Against: Does Your School Truly Put Student Learning First?**   **49**

    Teacher- Versus Learner-Centered Practices   50

    Creating a Sense of Urgency   52

    Faces of the Achievement Gap   52

    Own It!   52

5. **All-Star Performance: What Will Your Legacy Be? The Leadership Implications Of Systemic Change for All Students**   **55**

    Transformational Leaders as Agents of Change   55

    Own the Challenge   56

    The Soul of a Leader   57

    Conclusion   58

    Turning Points   59

Appendices

    Appendix A: Envisioning Life Beyond High School   61

    Appendix B: Demystifying College   65

    Appendix C: Life Skills   67

    Appendix D: Enrichment Opportunities   69

    Appendix E: Student Growth Plan   71

    Appendix F: Schoolwide Standards for Behavior   75

    Appendix G: Classroom Goals (Fifth-Grade Example)   79

    Appendix H: Dreamboard Template   81

    Appendix I: Hattie's Meta-Strategies for Student Growth   83

    Appendix J: My Plan for Success   85

    Appendix K: Grade Improvement Plan   87

    Appendix L: Levels of Support   89

References   **93**

Index   **99**

Preface

I am writing this book to ensure that the voices of students who are at risk of school failure do not go unheard. These students' needs must not get lost in our nation's narrow focus on test preparation and results-driven performance expectations. School leaders and support teams must make certain that caring relationships are established between adults and students. In addition, students need to be engaged at the school and classroom levels so they take ownership of their learning to increase their academic outcomes.

The purpose of the book is to offer classroom practitioners, support team specialists, and all levels of classroom and school leaders practical strategies and plays for their playbooks. They can then productively coach school teams and establish a full-court press on diverse student populations who have the largest number of risk factors.

There continues to be a need for a distinctive and more student-centered approach because current practices, policies, and structures have not adequately raised the achievement of disenfranchised students. In fact, the need has never been more momentous. Our troubled economy requires our future leaders and members of the workforce to be more specialized and adept at their crafts. Our students must develop unique skill sets that set them apart as innovators in extremely competitive applicant pools. In addition, despite countless local, district, and state measures and initiatives, our current systems fail to give students the scaffolded support they need to bounce back from risk and adversity. Educational leaders and support teams need to utilize more empirical and low-cost strategies to close achievement gaps and to allow students to rebound from risk.

This book will provide those concrete strategies that have been proven to be successful in schools across our country. In schools where resilience is fortified through caring relationships and engagement, students grow socially, emotionally, and academically. Their risk factors will still be present because there are many parts of a child's life that we cannot control or influence. However, educators can use structures and supports to ensure that all students, including those who are at risk, experience turning points in their classrooms and schools. It will not only detail school structures to boost achievement but will also describe the classroom benefits of implementing the strategies that forge strong adult–student relationships. Educators will improve their pedagogical practices as they learn ways to ensure that student participation is meaningful and connected to their lives.

All members of a school staff have to execute their revitalized game plans so that they will keep high levels of risk from sidelining players who belong in the starting lineup. Readers will finish the book armed with an arsenal to wage war on the achievement gaps in their classrooms, schools, districts, counties, states, or nation.

"The inspiration to dream and an abundance of hope cultivated by caring adults will together determine the endurance of a child's heart."

—Gabe Simon, EdD (2012)

About the Author

 **Gabe Simon, EdD,** has spent 18 years in education as a teacher and administrator. He earned all his graduate degrees from California State University Sacramento (master's degree in educational administration, and doctoral degree in transformational leadership). He is also a faculty member at California State University Sacramento and teaches quantitative and qualitative research methods to undergraduates in the education department. He has published regional and national articles on fortifying student hope and resilience through courageous student-centered leadership. This is his first book for school and classroom leaders and practitioners.

He enjoys playing and coaching soccer, playing tennis, swimming, and traveling with his two terrific children, Zachary and Amanda. He lives in Fair Oaks, California, and is currently a middle school principal at Creekview Ranch Middle School in the Dry Creek Joint Elementary School District.

This book is dedicated to all classroom and school trailblazers who urgently pursue student success. These educators and administrators do whatever it takes using the most student-centered and timely methods. They admit they do not have the answers to solve many problems. Nevertheless, despite fiscal challenges and dwindling resources, they relentlessly pursue best practices and implement them with courageous leadership. They tenaciously build resilience so that students can stare adversity in the face and say "Bring it on! I will overcome all obstacles." Positive deviance reigns supreme as they openly learn from the successes and failures of others.

Most important, I dedicate this work to my two children, Zachary and Amanda. You light the way for me, bring me joy, and build my resilience through your love, laughter, and energetic support. I love you both! Thank you to my parents, Gerry and Karolyn, for always reminding me that I am better and stronger than I believe myself to be through your support and actions.

I also have the utmost respect and admiration for all my close friends and colleagues who have been there through trying times and were always on the other side with open arms—*C. B.,* J. S., K. K., M. H., G. O., J. McL., C. N., Z. S., and S. C. You accept me for who I am and to put it simply, that is strong and courageous.

Thank you to Jessica Allan from Corwin for believing in the importance of this work and for being patient and positive. Finally, thank you to Evonne Rogers of the Dry Creek Joint Elementary School District for her terrific proofreading and insight.

John McLean: your spirit and the way you leaned into life live on and inspire!

Introduction

Turning Points

*Urgently Identifying the
Roadblocks to Student Success*

*"A school can create a coherent environment, a climate, more potent
than any single influence—teachers, class, family, neighborhood, so
potent that for at least six hours a day it can override almost everything
else in the lives of children."*

—Ron Edmonds (1986)

In the field of education, the essential question is still the following:
How do we propel students' academic trajectories upward especially
when working with our most at-risk students? Working toward this goal
becomes seemingly more difficult with fewer resources and an ever-
increasing level of local and federal accountability. Despite these challenges, this book will provide classroom practitioners, educators, support
staffs, specialists, and all levels of school administrators practical strategies and guidance to improve their daily work with diverse student populations. There is no one answer but there are extremely effective strategies
that assist students in navigating the treacherous trails of risk and adversity. This book will offer a unique perspective because it includes source
data from the students themselves. It is through these powerful voices that
the author offers usable tools and supports to improve student learning
and close achievement gaps among disenfranchised student subgroups.

These are tools that put all students in the starting lineup instead of leaving some on the bench.

Readers will learn about the power of establishing caring-connected relationships between adults and students in schools across our country. They will also discover how increasing student engagement can greatly improve student learning. Engaged and connected students simply learn at higher levels regardless of their risk factors, socioeconomic status, subgroup, or home life. There are many parts of a child's life that we cannot control or change. However, educators can use structures and supports to ensure that all students rebound from risk and experience turning points in their classrooms and schools. The reader will finish the book armed with an arsenal to wage war on the achievement gaps in his or her classroom, school, district, county, state, or nation.

OUR CURRENT LANDSCAPE

According to Thomas (2000) and Weinstein (2002), "Schools that serve large numbers of (economically) disadvantaged students are least likely to offer the types of instruction" and materials that give students the skills to meet rigorous academic standards (as cited in Becker & Luthar, 2002, p. 201). In addition, these students are more likely to receive negative feedback about their progress in school. Students who come from economically disadvantaged households are more likely to experience academic failure[1] and disengage from school experiences (p. 200). Failure may also include possible sanctions against these students disguised as "interventions" such as retention or unsuccessful promotion to the next grade level. In many schools, at-risk students[2] are educated in teacher-centered classrooms where there is little student engagement or ethic of caring.

As Figure I.1 clearly illustrates, our nation contributes far fewer funds to provide a highly effective education for students from high-poverty households than they are currently spending on defense costs (United States Government Spending, 2011).

---

[1] For the purposes of this publication, *academic failure* is defined as receiving failing or nonproficient academic achievement scores.

[2] For the purposes of this publication, *at-risk students* are defined by the author as those students who are at risk of academic failure. The author considers economically disadvantaged students, Hispanic, African-American, and students from other minority and disenfranchised groups at risk.

Figure I.1   Categories of Federal Spending in Billions of Dollars (2011)

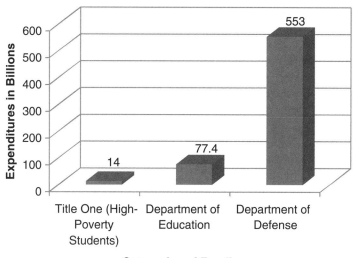

In fact, our nation spends over 7 times as much to fund our defense arsenal as it does in funding education and over 39 times more on defense than on funding for high-poverty students. According to Anyon (2005), the financial status of families living in poverty is related directly to the amount of funding that schools receive (as cited in Nevarez & Wood, 2007, p. 269). Therefore, it is not surprising that many states across the United States house a disproportionate number of high-poverty schools which are underfunded and often lack the appropriate resources for effective student supports.

Inequities in educational funding based on family income make it critical for schools and districts to locally address the needs of high-poverty schools and their students. These high-poverty institutions need to implement classroom strategies that will directly result in improved student outcomes to offset funding inequities. At-risk students will benefit from school-based protective factors such as caring-adult relationships and a high level of engagement. Students will experience academic success in the presence of these protective factors, and our nation will close the achievement gap. These factors build student resiliency or their ability to bounce back in the face of risk and adversity. Simply put, they are turning points in the turbulent lives of students who are at risk of school failure. We will revisit this concept in greater detail later in this chapter.

Despite countless improvement efforts such as sweeping educational reforms, No Child Left Behind legislation, and statewide accountability requirements to meet adequate yearly progress in language arts and math, the difference in achievement trends between disadvantaged and advantaged students still persists. Figure I.2 illustrates achievement disparities in eighth-grade reading over the last 13 years.

As the figure demonstrates, in 2011, 44 percent of eighth-grade students who were eligible for free and reduced lunch performed at or above the proficient level in reading on the National Assessment of Educational Progress. Another way to look at the same data is the following: in 2011, 56 percent of eighth-grade students who were eligible for free and reduced lunch were not proficient in reading. As Figure I.2 clearly shows, although high-poverty students have improved their achievement, nondisadvantaged students' scores have dropped. The reading achievement disparities persist in high school as well. Finally, in colleges across the nation, "only 9 percent of freshmen in the top colleges are from the bottom half" of the socioeconomic status distribution (McKinsey & Company, 2009, p. 12). In summary, high-poverty students frequently achieve at lower levels than nondisadvantaged students. They often graduate from high school lacking essential literacy skills and are less likely to attend top colleges and universities.

An achievement gap becomes more evident when focusing on specific states. California's achievement in language arts provides just one snapshot among a scrapbook of states with achievement disparities. When investigating achievement in California in the area of language arts, the data suggests a need for improved school and classroom practices when working with at-risk students. The gap in language arts for the 2011

Figure I.2 1998-2011 National Assessment of Educational Progress in Eighth-Grade Reading: Percentage at Proficient Level or Above

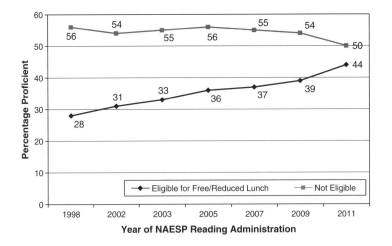

administration of the California Standards Test (CST) was 28 percent. More specifically, 44 percent of economically disadvantaged students scored proficient or advanced, while an average of 72 percent of students who were not economically disadvantaged scored proficient or advanced. We must urgently acknowledge these levels of proficiency as roadblocks to student success that can be avoided with strong a student-centered and resiliency-based full-court press.

REBOUNDS: RESILIENCY OVERVIEW

Educators face a daily, continual challenge to discover specific instructional and systemic methods that will narrow achievement gaps and create academic turning points for their students. In the current economic climate, they must boost achievement with limited resources, larger class sizes, and an ever changing accountability landscape. How do educators engage at-risk students through a journey of discovery instead of blazing ahead without them? The answers can be found in the study of resiliency, a theory and "belief in the ability of every person to overcome adversity if important resiliency protective factors are present" in their lives (Krovetz, 1999, p. 1). Resiliency studies assert that when people in a school community care about a student, hold high expectations for him or her, and provide "purposeful support," that student will rebound from risk and be able to conquer adversities in his or her life (p. 1). "Burns (1994) defines these resiliency protective factors as traits, conditions, or situations that alter or reverse potentially destructive outcomes" (Shepard, 2004, p. 210). Protective factors can be found in an environment where at least one adult cares deeply about the child and where expectations are clear and set high. Meaningful participation is another protective factor for resilient students as they are given key roles in their place of learning.

The strategies, templates, and tools in this book will not result in a lasting impact on student achievement without genuinely and clearly communicating high-adult expectations. As educators and administrators, we let students know how much we expect out of them through the quality of the work we ask them to produce in the classroom and what we expect them to learn. We also communicate our expectations by letting students know how high we feel they are capable of climbing among the mountain of learning objectives and myriad of assessments. Many feel that expectations are only verbally or consciously communicated. However, as the table below indicates, it is the presence or lack thereof of unconscious and nonverbal messages that have the most lasting impact on student motivation and learning behaviors.

Table I.1

Expectation	Nonverbal communication	Message that it sends the student
I am here to help you and expect you to succeed (with no excuses).	Proximity, smiles, genuine concern, dedicating time to individually support at-risk students	An adult expects me to do it and they will help if I can't. Failing is not an option this teacher is willing to accept.
I will listen, hear, and act, but I expect you to tell me when there is a need.	Eye contact, repeating what student says, a concrete action plan with timely results, dedicating teacher–student time to build individual relationships	If I need to ask for anything or tell an adult about anything at school or at home, he/she will hear me and take action.
I will call on you because I expect you to participate.	Redirection through body language, proximity, wait time, monitoring during independent practice, mutual accountability	I cannot opt out of learning, and I must participate. Adults at my school care more about my success than I care about failing.
I will give you multiple opportunities for success, but I expect you to be responsible, work hard, and not give up.	Nonverbal and verbal feedback that is specifically related to desired learning targets, wait time, being optimistic and hopeful, reaching different learning modalities	If I bomb a test or mess up an assignment, my teachers will allow me to learn from my mistakes and will give me another chance at success. Mistakes are opportunities for me to learn new things.

There are also what we call silent killers in common areas of school campuses and in classrooms resulting from adults having low expectations of students. These are deadly behaviors because they kill a student's love of learning and create barricades to resiliency and hope. These killers include the following:

- Students who are not required to participate daily in class discussions or questions

- Sarcasm that demeans students or puts them down (publicly or privately)

- Telling a student he or she cannot do something because he or she is not capable

- Not actively listening to student concerns or failure to attend to risk factors

- Not providing students multiple opportunities for success in the form of test retakes and assignment redo's

- Lack of specific feedback on assignments with opportunities for revision

School leaders must seek out these killers utilizing their own arsenals of consistent classroom walk-throughs accompanied by honest and direct student-centered conversations. In these conversations about low-adult expectations, school leaders must simply state the behavior of the adult and its negative impact on student learning. The leader must then direct the adult to change his or her practices. However, some conversations may only require an indirect or coaching conversation.

THE NEED FOR TURNING POINTS

The California Healthy Kids Survey (CHKS) is funded by the California Department of Education. This particular survey and others like it are used in many school districts and counties across the state and the nation to collect and analyze data on the at-risk behavior of fifth and seventh graders as well as data on student resiliency. The survey provides reliable and valid results across multiple settings and is acknowledged and well respected in the field of resiliency research. More specifically, the survey generates perception data on the caring relationships that students experience from adults at school, students' meaningful participation at school, and their level of "personal school connectedness" (WestEd, 2009, p. 14).

The 2008–2010 fifth grade elementary aggregate Healthy Kids Survey results include statewide information about these factors. The CHKS results indicate that 57 percent of students reported a high level of caring relationships at school but only 16 percent felt strongly that their participation was meaningful. The overall score for students' connectedness toward school indicated that 60 percent of the students surveyed felt personally connected to their schools. As Chapter 1 will clearly indicate, seminal and recent peer-reviewed research shows that resiliency factors in schools have a positive effect on student achievement. However, as evidenced in the data, there is cause for concern among educators when it comes to resiliency. *Too few students consistently report that the resiliency factors of caring adult–student relationships and student engagement are highly present at their schools.*

In addition, a large amount of previous studies have honed in on the lack of student progress and possible underlying reasons. Research from Delpit (1995), Deschenes, Cuban, & Tyack (2001), Lynn (2006), Nelson 2006, and Tierney, Hau, & Englar-Carlson (2006) has demonstrated that at-risk students have been marginalized because "their culture is different and often dismissed or devalued in the academic arena" (as cited in Morales, 2008, p. 3). In contrast, resiliency is an additive and proactive model where skills and assets are strengthened and rebuilt. Rather than reactions or referrals, students are enveloped in a web of support. Adults know and recognize every child personally by name or cultural background and understand the gifts they bring to their classrooms. To put it simply, students feel valued and perform at higher levels academically when resiliency is fostered in school settings.

This phenomenon of resiliency can be traced back 40 years but has been absent from the majority of recent research literature until the last 4 to 5 years. Gándara (1995) and her studies on impoverished Mexican Americans who are able to reach the highest levels of education in spite of poverty are viewed by some as seminal works in this field (as cited in Morales, 2008, p.2). In her work with the Puente Project, Gándara demonstrated how more Hispanic students became college bound through the persistence and mentoring of caring adults. However, more recently, Gándara updated the progress report on Hispanic achievement. Hispanic students make up a good portion of at-risk populations in America's schools. Today one in five of America's students are Hispanic yet this subgroup of students receives less than 7 percent of college degrees awarded each year (Gándara, 2009, p. 38). Data such as this should compel educators to understand the urgency needed to "address this new demographic challenge" along with the lower achievement of other disenfranchised subgroups for the sake of our country's at-risk students (p. 38). Resilience can be developed, but it is up to adults in a school community to coach students to a winning season and follow a closely articulated game plan (Brokenleg & Bockern, 2003, p. 23).

When personally investigating caring relationships, a survey instrument was developed to include student questions about the quality of their relationships with adults at school. This assessment also asked the students to evaluate their interactions with adults, in particular behaviors toward them such as caring, listening, empathy, praise, and humor or laughter. The remainder of the student survey questions centered on their level of engagement or participation in the classroom as well as school interactions and activities. The results were nothing short of amazing: students who reported a high level of caring relationships with adults at school and/or a high level of classroom engagement experienced great improvements in their academic outcomes in the form of boosted standardized test scores. These findings are supported by the research that will be reviewed in Chapter 1.

INCLUDING STUDENT VOICES IN THE GAME PLAN

It is incredible that we often forget that the answers to questions about how to improve student learning are right in front of us. They are in our classrooms, the cafeteria, and on the playground. There are answers to the following most heavily debated question in education: how can we get more students to be proficient as measured by standardized tests? These answers can be found by simply asking the students what helps them to be successful or what would help them to improve their academic achievement. Throughout the book, the voices of students are highlighted as well as strategies for ensuring that they help design the game plan for fortifying resiliency in schools.

THE SIGNIFICANCE OF THIS WORK

This publication adds to the 40 years of resiliency research with a unique contribution. Previous works have focused on school-level outcome data. This work stems from survey and individual students' test score data as well as qualitative data from student focus groups and interviews. This information brings the research to the individual student level, unlike previous works about resiliency and therefore provides a powerful and credible perspective. According to WestEd's (2002) facts sheet titled *Health Risks, Resilience, and the Academic Performance Index*, further work is needed "to determine how the characteristics of individual students are related to individual academic test scores" (Hanson & Austin, 2002, p. 2). A major difference between this research and past investigations is the emphasis on student perceptions about classroom and teacher practices as opposed to an evaluation of the overall school system's response to gaps in achievement. This publication validates previous studies and theories of organizational systemic change and will specifically show practitioners how to narrow achievement gaps in their classrooms and schools.

The focus on reducing risk and strengthening student learning is supported by other studies in child and human development, family structures, school effectiveness, and research on developing school communities. Caring relationships from adults establish safety and trust with students. At the same time, high teacher expectations serve to guide and challenge students to seek out high levels of achievement despite numerous risk factors. Students who are able to participate in a meaningful way in the classroom and in school foster responsible decision making and contribute to communities (Benard, 1991, p. 4).

This work provides new knowledge in the field of educational administration by demonstrating the strong and reliable connections between student perceptions about the resiliency protective factors and whether or not these perceptions are related to increases or decreases in students' language arts achievement. Educational administrators will be able to use the practical recommendations and strategies found in this book to hone their transformational leadership skills in ways that directly impact the learning of each and every student. This book's research and its recommendations will allow site and district administrators to widen the scope of their school improvement lenses to focus on targeted protective factors that may positively impact student achievement.

The practical applications that stem from the recommendations within this work will contribute to the urgent goal of eliminating the achievement gap between at-risk and low-risk students. As local educators and educational leaders strengthen their relationships with students and elevate their expectations for student success, more previously disenfranchised subgroups will experience language arts proficiency and improvements in other content areas. This book outlines protective factors and school supports that have the greatest impact on student learning. Leaders and their staffs can use this work as a resource and guide to strengthen the resiliency protective factors in their organizations. In doing so, they will ensure that effective conditions exist to promote student learning in every classroom.

1

How Do We Know They Will Bounce Back?

*"In order to succeed, people need a sense of self-efficacy, strung together
with resilience to meet the inevitable obstacles and inequities of life."*
—Albert Bandura

EVIDENCE FROM THE RECORD BOOKS

The academic information in this chapter provides the foundational
knowledge necessary to accurately and effectively improve student learning. This information is critical to fully comprehend the research base
behind formidable school and classroom solutions. Schools must demonstrate caring by engaging their students daily so that they can successfully
navigate the treacherous pathways of risk and low achievement. It is time
somebody told educators what works to improve student learning based
on the years of trailblazing research that is housed in this chapter. But
more important, in the words of teenage poet Quantedius Hall (2000), "it
is time somebody told" the students that adults in schools care and will do
whatever it takes for students to be successful (as cited in Franco, 2000, p.
1). Quantedius said much more than this in his pleading poem of survival,
hopes, and resiliency. His words should motivate you to read further in
this chapter and in this book to learn the research behind students who
rebound from risk. His words will also help educators determine how they
can positively impact students like him more consistently each day.

The essence of this chapter is a well researched list of recommendations that will assist schools in successfully conducting systemic change and fostering resiliency in order to improve student outcomes. To that end, we will begin with research-based information about the impact of school-level resiliency protective factors and a rationale for changing school practices to narrow achievement gaps. Important theoretical aspects of resiliency will be reviewed to properly frame the impact of protective factors on student outcomes. Seminal works on the long-term impact of building student resiliency are discussed along with studies on the protective factors shown to positively impact student achievement in language arts.

Resiliency research "provides the prevention, education, and youth development fields with nothing less than a fundamentally different knowledge base and paradigm for research and practice" (Benard, 1991, p. 5). Resiliency provides practitioners with optimism and an additive shelter as they approach student challenges with learning key content along with their battles through adversity. This paradigm focuses on the process of improving student learning and steers away from programmatic elements in school settings. "Ultimately resilience is a process of connectedness, of linking to people, to interests, and ultimately to life itself" (Benard, 1991, p. 6). Moving from risk to resilience empowers classroom practitioners and educational leaders to require social change within their organizations.

Creating structures so students can rebound from risk is critical because many schools where economically disadvantaged students attend still do not provide the needed academic, social, or emotional support that these students' challenges require. This subgroup's risk factors include a high degree of mobility, learning challenges, and dysfunctional families. These factors can significantly stand in the way of academic gains (Riley, 2006, p. 2). At-risk students are frequently assigned to the lowest classroom ability groups in elementary and middle schools (Becker & Luthar, 2002, p. 198). To make matters worse, research has shown that teachers' expectations of students are influenced by the student demographic variables of social class and ethnicity. These demographic variables illuminate racial and income discrepancies in achievement that get larger as students spend more time in school (The Future of Children, 2005, as cited in Hughes & Kwok, 2007, p. 39).

Children from households in poverty score as much as 60 percent lower in "cognitive performance than middle-income children their age" (Neuman, 2009, as cited in Midcontinent Research for Education and Learning [McRel], 2010, p. 30). More specifically, children in poverty arrive in kindergarten having seen and heard 30 million fewer words than many children from middle-income backgrounds (Neuman, 2009, as cited in McRel, 2010, p. 30). What matters most in educating children in poverty and other disenfranchised student subgroups is the guarantee of "challenging, engaging, and intentional instruction" (McRel, 2010, p. 67). Barriers to learning extend beyond test scores. Roadblocks for at-risk youth come in the form of disengagement, low expectations, and a lack of supportive relationships between adults and children on school campuses. Little attention has been paid in recent reforms to removing those barriers that are related to a school's culture and climate.

Currently, many urban settings that house the most at-risk students have a high teacher turnover rate and typically the least qualified staff to deliver instruction. It is more important than ever to look for low-cost or no-cost ways to improve student learning with the current financial constraints of an uncertain economic future regionally and nationally. Building resiliency focuses on what teachers say and do in their daily interactions with students and provides a solution-oriented framework. Teachers and districts do not need to spend a great deal of monies to improve student learning. Again, what matters most for these students are engaging classrooms that foster supportive and caring relationships with all students (McRel, 2010, p. 67).

Darling-Hammond (2000) discusses the critical need for a change in the way we educate students in the United States. In a strong statement, she proposes that current school systems need to change to effectively address the needs of diverse students. Higher standards alone "will not enable them to learn" (p. 1). Building resiliency is crucial as students who live in high-poverty households are exposed to poverty-related stress (Wadsworth & Santiago, 2008, p. 406). This stress has a negative impact on these students' degree of resiliency and can "hinder the development of effective coping abilities" (p. 406).

The key resiliency protective factors provide educators with ways to effectively harness the interpersonal skills and creative strengths of their students. With deliberate adjustments to instructional delivery and greater and more meaningful student interactions student learning will improve.

THE IMPACT OF THE RESILIENCY PROTECTIVE FACTORS

In their study of kindergarten classrooms, Ponitz, Rimm-Kaufmann, Grimm, and Curby (2009) discovered that classrooms where students were effectively engaged with "rich, positive interactions" were predictive of improved literacy achievement (p. 102). These researchers refer to recent studies from Connor et al. (2005) and Mashburn et al. (2008) that indicate that "the actual daily interactions among teachers and students in the class-room most strongly predict achievement" (as cited in Ponitz et al., p. 103).

When speaking to the positive effect of caring adult relationships, Ponitz et al. (2009) acknowledge the link between building connections with students and instructional effectiveness. Social and academic challenges can be addressed "by interacting with children in engaging, interesting, and positive ways" (p. 104). When children become engaged in their classrooms, learning improves. They conclude their study further emphasizing the strong correlation between engaging instructional practices and reading achievement (p. 117).

Voices From the Classroom: Examples of this interactive relationship included the following (from the students' perspectives):

- "They help us."
- "Teachers are nice to us."
- "They are good listeners."
- "They encourage us."
- "They use good eye contact when they talk to us."
- "They fix our problems."
- "We can trust teachers."
- "They respect us."
- "They won't tell anyone about what we talk about."
- "Teachers ask about our home life."

Martin and Dowson (2009) speak to students' relationships at school with adults and the critical role these relationships play in improving student engagement. They cite numerous studies to support these conclusions (Ainley, 1995; Battistich & Hom, 1997; Hargreaves, Earl, & Ryan, 1996; Pianta, 1998). Martin and Dowson (2009) discuss "connective instruction," which relates learning to students' experiences and needs in order to foster motivation and high levels of engagement (p. 344). They offer further evidence of the power of caring adult relationships through their review of previous research in this area (Goodenow, 1993; Teven & McCroskey, 1997; Connell & Wellborn, 1991).

"Addressing the (emotional) health . . . needs of youth is a critical component of a comprehensive strategy" to improve student achievement (Hanson, Austin, & Lee-Bayha, 2004, p. 14). Protective factors supported by resiliency research will help educators fulfill the necessary commitment of learning for all students. They will also assist schools in closing achievement gaps that persist in our current deficit-driven system. At-risk students will be supported from all levels of a school's support system when caring and dedicated adults engage them in learning and ensure they can successfully navigate risk and bounce back from adversity.

SUMMARY OF THEORETICAL BASE

Resiliency Theory

The theory of resiliency was originally known as the *Resilience Cycle* and includes the key elements of needs assessments, protective factors, and the development of a student's internal locus of control (Morales, 2008, p. 23). Students who are academically resilient achieve despite overwhelming statistics that have historically proven otherwise. Research and theories have often focused on student failure and have followed a deficit model. In contrast, resiliency theory is additive in that it states that if protective factors such as caring adult relationships, high teacher expectations, and student engagement are introduced and consistently practiced, students from marginalized subgroups can beat the odds and experience academic success.

According to Bonnie Benard (1991), resiliency research is supported by other studies in child and human development, family structures, school effectiveness, and research on developing school communities. Caring relationships from adults establish safety and trust with students despite numerous risk factors. Students who are able to participate in a meaningful way in the classroom and in school foster responsible decision making and contribute to communities (Benard, 1991, p. 4).

> *The fastest way to fail is to improve on yesterday's successes.*
> —W. Edwards Deming
> (as cited in Kuykendall, 2004)

Leadership Theory of Social Justice

A transformative leadership style is built from a solid foundation of respect, caring, recognition, and empathetic practices. When leaders who promote social justice were studied, they consistently worked to create socially and culturally response educational settings for all students (Theoharis, 2007, p. 223). Leaders advanced their initiatives toward social justice to raise student achievement and close the achievement gap between disadvantaged and advantaged students. School structures of student support were strengthened, the staff's capacities to successfully navigate positive change was improved, and school cultures were fortified (p. 232).

Principals who became successful leaders of social justice reforms in their schools were proactive in their approaches. Their preemptive strategies for school change included purposeful communication, developing a network of supportive administrators, keeping focused on their goals, prioritizing their efforts, immersing themselves in professional learning, and finally building strong interpersonal relationships with staff members.

The leadership theory of social justice clearly notes that most change efforts are met with some forms of resistance. This resistance includes competing district office initiatives and staff members whose core values conflict with a site or district's student-centered direction. Theoharis (2007) states that administrators must be on the front lines in the battle to transformationally lead and change schools (p. 250). The theory states that leaders must develop a "reflective consciousness" for social justice that includes equity and justice, a deeper knowledge of self, and the belief that the dream of equitable instruction and instructional systems is possible (Scheurich & Skrla, 2003; Rapp, 2002; as cited in Theoharis, 2007, p. 250).

The theory of social justice leadership makes clear distinctions between good leaders and social justice leaders. While good leaders support programs for diverse learners, leaders for social justice focus on strengthening core instructional methods and curriculum. They also ensure that all students have similar access to the core program in schools (Theoharis, 2007, p. 252). Good leaders empower teachers but leaders for social justice require success for all students and collaboratively meet in a timely manner to problem solve how all students will achieve that success.

SEMINAL WORK ON RESILIENCE: THE KAUAI STUDY

Werner and Smith (as cited in Benard, 2004) completed what has been often called the seminal work in studying risk and resilience. They conducted research on over 700 children, many who had up to four high-risk factors. The researchers followed the progress of these children from birth to adulthood over 40 years. Known as the *Kauai study*, this research demonstrated that at-risk children who receive a great deal of support and modeling from low-risk adults and youth beat the odds and become responsible citizens. The longitudinal study combined case study accounts and statistical analyses to investigate the impact of biological and social risk factors on the participants' development and coping abilities. Werner and Smith concluded that only one out of six of the study's sample was struggling with problems ranging from financial issues, violence, substance abuse, or mental health issues 40 years later (p. 7). All the study participants were born in Kauai in 1955, and the longitudinal data was collected three times during their lives.

The impact of protective factors was determined by Werner and Smith as more profound than the impact of risk factors or significant negative life experiences or events. They state that the supports known as *resiliency protective factors* apply to all young people who face adversity in addition to simply those at risk of school failure. These protective factors include working on social skills, having a caring and committed caregiver, and having a community support system that may include schools or churches. They further explain resilience as using "self-righting tendencies" to help children develop normally even when they experience the highest levels of adversity in their lives (Benard, 2004, p. 9). These researchers also cite the importance of developing children's internal locus of control or their "personal power" (p. 22). They were among the first researchers to identify hope and confidence as central to the lives of resilient people.

The authors of the Kauai study conclude their research with recommendations to school personnel to foster student resilience. Their primary recommendation was for educators to continue being positive role models for youth. They concluded by asking educators to share "the gift of hope" with all students to develop trust, initiative, and competence (WestEd, 2001, p. 23). We will revisit this recommendation of increased student engagement and its impact on achievement later in this chapter.

SPECIFIC RESILIENCY PROTECTIVE FACTORS IMPACTING STUDENT ACHIEVEMENT

The Impact of Caring Adults

The resiliency protective factor of caring adults in students' lives has been shown to positively impact students' academic outcomes. Noddings (1992) identified caring as "the very bedrock of all successful education" (as cited in Lumpkin, 2007, p. 158). Noddings also identified that a strength of caring teachers was their ability to reflect on and refine teaching practices to meet the needs of every student. In *Changing the Odds* (2010), the Midcontinent Research for Education and Learning concluded that fostering meaningful relationships with students that were also nurturing and strong were qualities of effective teaching practices (p. 18).

Voices From the Classroom:

Students also perceived the school support of caring adults through the lens of the expectations they had for them at school. Unfortunately, students gave less detail about these expectations than the previous lively descriptions about caring adult-teacher interactions. Examples of these expectations included the following:

- "We are rewarded for doing good work."
- "Teachers encourage us to do our best."
- "If we do quality work, we are praised."
- "They tell us to never give up with our work."

According to Pianta, Belsky, Vandergrift, Houts, and Morrison (2008), in addition to instructional aspects of classrooms, there is evidence that emotional classroom aspects are "predictive of gains in achievement" (p. 367). The quality of the adult and student interaction is the biggest determinant of success (Noam & Fiore, 2004, p. 9). Resiliency research demonstrates the huge significance of adults as mentors and role models especially for educationally or socioeconomically disadvantaged students (p. 10). Research has found that African-American and socioeconomically disadvantaged students are less likely than Caucasian or advantaged students to experience supportive relationships with teachers (Entwisle & Alexander, 1988; Hamre & Pianta, 2001; Ladd et al., 1999; Wehlage & Rutter, 1986, as cited in Hughes & Kwok, 2007, p. 40).

Noam and Fiore (2004) feel that relational practices and tools can be developed further through teacher training and work with school-learning environments. They conclude by stating the following: "The foundations have been laid in theory, research, and promising practices. Now the institutional changes have to follow" (p. 14).

Hattie's (2009) synthesis of over 800 meta-analyses and 500,000 studies related to what impacts student achievement offers further evidence of the significance of the teacher-student relationship. Hattie cites Cornelius-White's (2007) meta-analysis of 119 studies, 1,450 effects, 355,325 students, 14,851 teachers, and 2,439 schools (p. 118). Cornelius-White found a strong correlation (.34) between all teacher variables and all student outcomes. This researcher concluded from his analysis of numerous studies that teachers must facilitate student learning by showing that they care about each student's learning and each student as a person, "which sends a powerful message about purpose and priority" (Cornelius-White, as cited in Hattie, 2009, p. 119).

In the appendix of Hattie's (2009) research synthesis, the influence of the school, classroom, and family factors he reviewed were rank ordered by their positive influence on student achievement. Out of 138 influences on student achievement from multiple domains, teacher–student relationships ranked 11th with an effect size of .72 (Hattie, Appendix I). Looking at this information from another perspective, I concluded from Hattie's synthesis that teacher–student relationships have a greater impact on student achievement than 92 percent of the other influences in the over 800 analyses that Hattie reviewed. More specifically, the following influences mentioned in this study had a less significant impact on achievement: family socioeconomic status (d=.57), parental involvement (.51), student engagement (.48), teacher expectations (.43), gender (.12), and overall teacher effects (.32).

Table 1.1 summarizes current research on the resiliency protective factor of caring adult–student relationships and can be used to substantiate change efforts.

Table 1.1

Researchers	Study Participants	Major Conclusions	Applications
Hamre & Pianta (2001)	179 children studied from first through eighth grade	Students who had negative relationships with teachers had poor study habits and achievement	Students who have caring relationships with adults at school will experience increased academic achievement; interventions should be preventative
Worthy, Patterson, Salas, Prater, & Turner (2002)	24 struggling readers in grades 3 through 5	Social interactions with caring adults increased these students' interest in reading, motivation, and reading achievement	Reaching the most difficult students requires responsiveness from an adult with close and trusting connections to the student
Pianta & Stuhlman (2004)	490 children in preschool through first grade	Teachers noted higher achievement for children they had closer relationships with	Intervene early in the social and academic lives of at-risk students, establish close caring relationships at school with students
Hamre & Pianta (2005)	Student observations from 827 classrooms, 747 schools, and 32 states	High-risk (economically disadvantaged) kindergarten students who received emotional support from teachers maintained high test scores	Encourage students to be responsible for their own learning; give high-quality feedback to students, and engage students in the learning process frequently; simple adult–student interactions can have powerful effects on student outcomes

(Continued)

Table 1.1 (Continued)

Researchers	Study Participants	Major Conclusions	Applications
Hughes & Kwok (2007)	443 first-grade high-poverty low readers	Students who had stronger relationships with their teachers were more engaged and had higher achievement	Social relatedness is crucial for academic success, provide training for teachers on building warm and supportive relationships with their students
O'Connor & McCartney (2007)	1,364 preschool through first-grade children	Achievement is influenced by effective teacher communication and relationship quality	Focus on instructional interactions but also enhance relational interactions over time, focus interventions on improving teacher–student relationships
Liew, Chen, & Hughes (2010)	761 low-income and minority first graders	Strong teacher–student relationships allow students to self-regulate their motivation and achievement	Strong relationships allow students to compensate for academic difficulties, investing early in at-risk students pays dividends in their future achievement

Meaningful Student Participation

More and more students drop out of school because they do not see the value in getting an education. Furthermore, students who fail to finish high school will earn $16,000 less annually (U.S. Department of Education, 2007, p. 1). In 2007, the dropout rate was 10 times greater for students living in low-income families than their peers from high-income families (p. 4).

Clearly, an education is crucial for all students, especially those students from disadvantaged households. But improving the academic performance of students "requires that all schools work to more effectively engage all students" but especially students whose backgrounds have traditionally placed them at risk of school failure (Battistich, Watson, & Solomon, 1999, p. 418). Engaging students must mean providing them the skills to learn or to become more efficient self-directed learners. Meaningful participation is synonymous with engagement for the purposes of this book and is defined by Jennings (2003) as "the involvement of the student in relevant, engaging, and interesting activities with opportunities for responsibility and contribution" (p. 45).

Battistich, Watson, and Solomon (1999) conclude their research article with practical recommendations for practitioners to create classrooms that bear a greater resemblance to engaged communities. Some of these recommendations include increasing the amount of collaboration between students, actively involving students in classroom decision making, engaging student interests, and clearly explaining "the relevance of learning tasks" (p. 422). These researchers recommend that teachers take a "believing stance," which involves believing that students want to become part of a caring and engaged classroom community. It also requires ensuring that students desire to learn when given ownership and purpose (p. 425). If meaningful participation is increased for students in the classroom setting, teachers and administrators can expect to observe students who are more interested in learning, who have increased effort and persistence, who actively collaborate with the teacher to solve problems, and who take time and pride in their academic work. The inadequacies of our current education system must be confronted, and educators need to develop a complete range of student abilities and skills for them to fully and effectively engage in learning.

Table 1.2

Researchers	Study Participants	Major Conclusions	Applications
Greenwood, Horton, & Utley (2002)	64 kindergarten through fifth-grade teachers in 22 schools, 256 students	Students responded more when given more opportunities for writing and reading, reading instruction speeds up task management, students spent 42 percent of classroom time watching the teacher	Alternatives to whole-class instruction and lecture: peer tutoring, peer-to-peer interaction, computer-assisted instruction
Hanson, Austin, & Lee-Bayha (2004)	628 schools	Test scores and grades increased in schools where students indicated they had meaningful participation in the school community and decreased when engagement was low	Students are required to set short- and long-term goals, are mutually accountable for responding in class, and have a role in developing classroom rules and procedures; students are doing the learning over 50 percent of the instructional time

Hughes, Luo, Kwok, & Lloyd (2008)	2 first-grade cohorts of high-poverty students	Teachers who engaged their students also assisted in developing caring teacher–student relationships that led to higher math achievement; students supported by caring adults were more engaged, showed perseverance, were more open to feedback, and had better coping skills; reading achievement also improved with high levels of caring relationships and engagement	Improving student engagement in the classroom helps strengthen the impact of relationships on reading and math achievement; early classroom experiences should be engaging and should include a high level of teacher support
Ladd & Dinella (2009)	383 first-through third-grade students over 8 years	Teacher reports of cooperative students was positively correlated with higher student outcomes, higher student participation more strongly predicted achievement gains	By increasing the levels of student engagement, schools can predict long-term academic growth for their students, and students progress more consistently; engagement should be emphasized in school interventions

Classroom Connections:

Teachers who facilitated student-to-student small-group interactions left the strongest impression on student language arts test scores. The student voices provided examples of adult engagement strategies that included the following:

- Making learning fun
- "They teach us in ways that make us understand what we are learning."
- "They check in with us to make sure we understand what they taught."
- "They allow us to write to express ourselves and to solve problems."

Recent Studies: Student Engagement

Table 1.2 summarizes current research on engagement's role in improving student outcomes and includes practical applications for schools, classrooms, and other systems of student support.

CONCLUSION

There is hope to be found in fostering resiliency in at-risk students. However, it is a reform that requires systemic change. This change centers around the belief that what adults do around children each day makes a monumental difference in their lives (Krovetz, 1999, p. 3). Supports and opportunities need to address students' emotional, motivational, and social needs as well as their academic needs. Schools can develop resilience through fostering mentoring relationships with students. They must build academic and social connections daily with a high level of cooperative learning processes and with the support to make learning happen. Students require multiple opportunities for engagement and participation in classrooms. Learner-centered practices such as emphasizing choice and differentiating instruction engage students in their learning and build their "academic self-confidence" (p. 163).

The remainder of this book provides the specific tools educators need to significantly mitigate student risk factors. It will provide school leaders and classroom practitioners with an array of strategies to initiate more student-centered activities and change while improving academic outcomes. Each school and classroom must select the strategies that provide the best fit for their student population and that support the level of urgency needed to narrow achievement gaps. Are you ready to bring your A game?

2 The Caring School Team

The Schoolwide Game Plan

"Maybe before we didn't know,
That Corey is afraid to go
To school, the store, to roller skate.
He cries a lot for a boy of eight.
But now we know each day it's true
That other girls and boys cry too.
They cry for us to lend a hand.
Time for us to take a stand. . ."

"And tonight, some child will go to bed,
No food, no place to lay their head.
No hand to hold, no lap to sit,
To give slobbery kisses, from slobbery lips.
So you and I we must succeed
In this crusade, this holy deed,
To say to the children in this land:
Have hope. We're here. We take a stand!"

—Geoffrey Canada, 1996

STUDENTS' PERSPECTIVES ON SUPPORT

The previous chapters have diagrammed the power of the full-court press of caring adult–student relationships coupled with student engagement. These relationships also afford students protection from the negative impact of risk factors, and they strengthen their ability to rebound from risk. Years of peer-reviewed research support the data that was obtained from student interviews of focus groups and individual students in an elementary school setting. Students were asked what they need from caring adults and how those adults support them in school. The supportive climates that students describe in this chapter seem very straightforward and should be easy to build or replicate. However, they are rarely found in many schools across the country, especially in those schools with the largest achievement gaps and most diverse student populations.

This investigation into the impact of protective factors on student learning began with student responses from a fourth- and fifth-grade survey about the level of caring at their schools. Then complex statistics were run that investigated the relationship between high levels of caring and student language arts achievement on standardized tests. The results were powerful, statistically significant, and supported by the research that was reviewed in previous chapters. Students who noted high levels of caring from adults at their school experienced an increase in their test scores. More specifically, the presence of caring adults in the school setting predicted an average positive test score variability of 23 scaled score points with 96.3 percent (1–.027) confidence. For every value of the variable that measures a high level of caring in school, we can be 95 percent confident that a student's test score will increase between 3 and 43 points. In simpler terms, students have the potential to increase their language arts proficiency by one or more levels when adults show them that they care.

What did the students report when they were asked for more information about the caring adults in their schools? In their relationships with these adults, students cited many examples of how caring was communicated in their schools mainly by their teachers, campus supervisors, and administrators. Adults helped the students at recess with peer conflicts and problem solving. More precisely, student problem-solving support came in the form of specifically praising students for making learning-centered choices, teachers persisting with questioning strategies, challenging students academically, and encouraging students to increase their effort and participation.

Caring Teacher Supports:

Caring adult–student practices improve the learning of the most at-risk students. Students whose teachers noticed they were absent had higher test scores, particularly special education students. At-risk students must feel like they have some unique talents to contribute to the overall efficiency of their classroom. Students' spirits seemed to visibly illuminate when they described teacher supports.

Interpersonally, teachers gave the students solid eye contact and demonstrated active listening. Students described climates of trust, respect, confidentiality, and kindness. These interactions seem so basic but are often overlooked or ignored because of large class sizes, fast pacing of the curriculum, and broken systems of support that focus on outcomes rather than on strengthening the human factor of caring relationships.

Caring was also demonstrated when students appeared bothered or upset about something in school. Students cited support with playground problems and peer conflicts. They also felt comfortable that they would receive teacher assistance when they experienced academic struggles. Students who were bothered about stress from home factors were counseled effectively by caring teachers. Some of these home factors included divorce, a death in the family, the emotional problems of siblings, and lack of financial resources within their families.

Voices From the Classroom:

Students provided the most diverse examples when describing how they felt like they were part of their school through engaging programs and activities. Student assemblies, clubs (clay and German clubs), guest speakers, activities (spelling bees and plays), and classroom jobs all gave students a feeling of ownership and connectedness to their schools. Students became the most animated when they described the engaging elements of their schools.

Students also described how adults encouraged them to get involved at school and to increase their engagement in the school setting. Students used interactive journals and class meetings to solve problems. Adults asked students for suggestions when developing school rules or when teachers were deciding how to deliver essential content. Teachers engaged the students in purposeful dialogue about their home lives and time spent outside of school. The common theme when it came to engagement was student centeredness and teacher flexibility. Those elements were essential for students to feel engaged and consequently to experience academic growth and resiliency.

I have described necessary teacher interpersonal qualities and interactions for caring adult–student relationships and academic growth. But what are some specific and practical ways in the trenches every day that adults can protect students from risk and cover them in a web of support? Listed below are some examples that foster resiliency and hope and reduce student risk.

Caring as a Schoolwide Web of Support

Bonnie Benard (2004) provides specific strategies of how schools can effectively wrap their web of support around students who have varying levels of risk factors to improve student achievement. These school supports are captured in Table 2.1 and can be implemented through student-centered staff dialogue along with a systemic effort to foster a more positive climate and culture. Schools that are able to move "from risk to resilience are characterized" by the dimensions listed below (p. 87). As Noddings (1988) stated, the positive development of youth and academic success should work harmoniously instead of being in competition with each other (p. 32 as cited in Benard, 2004, p. 86). She so eloquently explained that caring has deteriorated in schools, but when "schools focus on what really matters in life, the cognitive ends we now pursue so painfully and artificially will be achieved more naturally" (Noddings, 1988, p. 32 as cited in Benard, 2004, p. 86).

Each successful school's web of support is cast with the understanding that educators must take responsibility for all children, especially those who are at the greatest risk for school failure. These students can be the toughest to love, invest time in, and support. However, when educators take a strength-based approach to celebrate all wins, big and small, learning becomes an emphatic slam dunk.

Table 2.1

The Game Plan: The Schoolwide "Web of Caring Support"

A Caring School Has the Following Elements in Place or Under Construction:

❏ Creates and sustains a caring climate through positive and genuine adult–student interactions

❏ Requires students to envision their future and lives beyond high school (see Appendix A for examples)

❏ Demystifies the college experience so students can plot their courses for their futures and dream big (see Appendix B)

❏ A staff that is available and responsive to all student needs

❏ Fosters respect and common courtesy (life skills: see Appendix C for examples)

❏ Provides means for students to disclose information and/or thoughts about the presence of risk at home and in their lives

❏ Possesses a school climate that is nonjudgmental and action oriented

❏ The system of support is flexible based on student needs and backgrounds

❏ Community-building processes exist to build bridges between families, communities, and schools

❏ Peer-support structures are in place

❏ Cross-age mentors are used (older students and/or community members)

❏ Resources are readily available (educational, cultural, employment, recreational, health, and social services)

❏ The physical environment is clean and well maintained

❏ Student work is displayed in common areas

❏ Service learning occurs through cooperative student groups

❏ The cultures of all students are evident

❏ Enrichment opportunities are available for students (see Appendix D for examples)

❏ Students are challenged to think critically and use an inquiry-based approach

❏ Rewards become intrinsic

❏ Students are actively involved in schoolwide decision making

Source: Adapted from Weinstein (1991).

Caring Through Supportive Persistence

The ethic of caring from adults can be measured on school campuses and needs to be greatly improved on many of them. When it comes to school failure, many students have been caught in a cycle of letdowns and dead ends. Some work hard to intentionally fail and disrupt learning environments. To turn this around, educators have to purposefully work harder for student success than students are working at failure. This seems simple, but too often a narrow action plan leads to dead ends and little or no academic improvement for students. The systems in schools must band together, pool resources, and mobilize any and all energies in and out of the school to require at-risk students to be cared for and engaged. The urgency is too great not to act in this manner and the stakes are too high.

To more effectively communicate that our school was a caring community through student-centered action, staff members identified students who were below proficiency on local and state measures. Our staff also used data on the risk factors of poor attendance and behavior to target students for relationship building. Teachers spent more time with these students during lunch and before and after school learning about their backgrounds, hopes, and dreams.

Our school support team challenged 45 of our most at-risk students to improve their behavior and grades. Counselors, administrators, teachers, aides, and clerical staff all supported them by celebrating their

Figure 2.1

My Plan for Success

CRMS

1-30-12

Student's Name Kai

Goal:
List something you would like to accomplish in the next 3 weeks.
Get at least a "C" in science

Help:
List qualities or characteristics you have that are strengths. These things will help you reach you reach your goal. (example: courage, social talent, independence, etc.)

☒ intelligence

☒ personallity

☒

☒

Figure 2.2

My Plan for Success

CRMS

Hang Ups:
List qualities or characteristics about you that could stand in the way of you reaching your goal. (example: angry sometimes, don't like to write, not good at math)

☒ Cell phone

☒ Computer

☒ Video games

☒ Going to the Gym everyday

Strategies for achieving this goal:

Step to Take	When?
Studying for test	Now
Turn in missing assignments	Now

Parent Signature Phone conference GS   Date 1-30-12

Student Signature Kai   Date 1-30-12

Admin/Counseling Signature Mr. Simon   Date 1-30-12

personal strengths and by helping them to confront the roadblocks to reaching their goals. These roadblocks included family dynamics, issues with self-esteem, and exposure to trauma. We collaboratively filled out a growth plan called "My Plan for Success" (see Appendix J) with each student and later used a weekly schedule for checking in with caring adults at school about the plan in our advisory classes (see Appendix E). The Plan for Success pictured opposite in Figures 2.1 and 2.2 is from a seventh grader named Kai.

Kai was failing his science class. He was capable of meeting standards yet lacked the motivation and follow through to realize his true potential. As the plan indicates, he committed to using his intelligence and outgoing personality to rally support at home and in school for his class work. He was also very honest about his hang-ups, which included playing too many video games, texting at all hours of the night, and getting distracted by spending too much time at the gym (he loves to practice and play basketball). Kai noted two specific actions he would take to raise his science grade, and 3 weeks later his plan was realized. Kai raised his grade to a 75 percent. His confidence was boosted, and his achievement in other classes improved as well. Kai is promoting to high school to continue his high level of success. He has also become the most inspirational and skilled player on his basketball team because of his renewed positive spirit, leadership, and improved mentoring capacity. This success story is just one example of how caring adults can do amazing things for students through interpersonal goal setting, consistent caring, and targeted action planning.

Our two terrific counselors identified students who were described as intentional nonlearners or students who were choosing to fail. They preferred to use a "Grade Improvement Plan" (see Appendix K) for these students. The plan was signed by the student, parent, counselor, and administration. This plan gave the student direction and hope, because it included the commitments of many adults on campus. The majority of these students began completing work and raising their grade point averages. Their promotion rates greatly improved as did their self-esteem, grades, and contributions to our school community. The strengthened and more focused presence of caring adults on our campus improved our school climate and student learning.

The Student Factor

When asking for input on school processes, supports, or programs, school leaders often work exclusively with adults. However, the student voice must be heard. If you are wondering whether or not your school is a caring school, just ask the students. They are the greatest measure of protective factors and provide subsistence to improve their own learning.

To improve the ethic of caring at our schools, we revitalized the quality of relationships between students and staff members at the middle and elementary school levels. Staff members reviewed peer-reviewed research that demonstrated how caring adult–student relationships have resulted in improved academic success (Pianta, Benard, & Morales). Using standardized testing data and local measures, students who were below proficiency in language arts and/or math were identified. These students needed staff to give them hope and mentoring but were often not vocal about their needs. Therefore, they were given a way to articulate their needs. Each staff member adopted and mentored three to five targeted students. Administration, office staff, and other support staff also joined in, and staff members received a small reimbursable budget for activities with their mentees. Some of these informal and caring connections included snacks with students, lunch, sports and physical education activities, weekly check ins, homework support, and providing gym and school clothing or school spirit wear for students in need.

Hope is hard to measure, but it skyrocketed among these students in the form of academic improvements and increased student involvement in extracurricular activities. Annual student surveys demonstrated that more and more children felt that adults cared about them. These caring adults were also able to get students involved in their own learning. The overall school climate was again transformed as teachers and support staff demonstrated increased commitments to fostering student-centered practices.

Caring Through Parent and Family Persistence

Many students who are at risk of school failure begin their journey with the cards seemingly stacked against them. Some come from single-parent households. Others may reside with other guardians or foster parents. Some are exposed to the toxins that are created by physical, emotional, and sexual abuse, or neglect. Others have lacked strong caring attachments to anything other than square Technicolor boxes and interactive remote controls. The odds that children who are exposed to these risk factors will be academically successful do not seem very likely. However, the resiliency of children can be fortified by caring and persistent adults in schools who raise the bar and require at-risk youth to rise above their dire circumstances.

Within the walls of a caring school, adults can develop partnerships with even the most dysfunctional families to bridge the gap between home and school. These partnerships allow the child to see that there are many adults in his or her life who not only want him or her to be successful but will require it. In my years of teaching and school administration, I have yet to find a parent, guardian, or family who I cannot get in contact with. The tenacity of the adults in schools will determine how strongly the bond between home and school is cemented. If all the family's contact numbers are disconnected and mailboxes are full, take another staff member with you and go on a field trip! Home visits send the message to a family that you care and that schools will do whatever it takes to keep a child from failing. Educate the family member(s) on how they can engage in school activities and provide some parent education resources specifically targeted to the greatest area of need for the child.

The following strategies are ways that parents and families can be encouraged to raise the level of caring in their homes so that children can focus on learning in schools instead of roadblocks to success (adapted from Weinstein, 1991):

- Create more one-on-one time with their child. If there are siblings, each one can have 30 to 60 minutes per week of a guardian's undivided attention (board games, hikes, etc.)
- Check in often (Who is the child talking to, texting with? What is he or she doing on the computer or phone? Where is the child during unsupervised times?)
- Get to know his or her hopes and dreams (see Appendices E, G, H, and J) for goal-setting and dream-building resources)
- Accept the child for who he or she is and not who others want him or her to be
- Encourage the child to connect to other caring and safe adults in the neighborhood
- Teach that mistakes provide lessons to learn and grow from
- Challenge and support the child (You should try, and I will help you do it.)
- Constantly communicate hope and optimism through positive and realistic messaging
- Choose the battles to fight—what is the importance of this issue for the child's academic and social successes in the short- and long-term?
- Consequences should be more natural and not too punitive

- Give the child responsibilities that are meaningful and focus on life skills
- Tap into local agencies for low- or no-cost activities and experiences (park and recreation departments, police and fire, boys or girls clubs)

Intelligently Caring

Social and emotional intelligences are crucial to student success. Strategies for boosting these skills may include increasing student awareness of feelings and what peers think about them (Benard, 2004, p. 165). "Learning to cooperate, resist negative peer pressure, and negotiate conflicts" are key proficiencies for at-risk students (p. 165). Teamwork and equal status in the classroom empower at-risk students as key members of that community. Planning and implementing activities through the lens of multiple intelligences allows students to demonstrate "their many ways of knowing" (Shepard, 2004, p. 213). For example, students who need hands-on and physical learning experiences should use manipulatives or movement to demonstrate their understanding.

Voices From the Classroom:

Students said they were the most engaged in small-group learning during language arts or reading blocks. They reported about half of the level of engagement for math as they did for language arts. Science and social studies provided students with the least amount of small-group interactions. However, students reported significantly lower levels of engagement when asked about writing opportunities. These writing opportunities may lead to increased student engagement and improved skills in critical thinking.

Additionally, their interpersonal intelligences can be validated through cooperative grouping strategies or mentoring programs. Also, specific praise from a teacher gives students signals that they are safe and important (Embry, 1997, p. 3). After all, feedback to students is the most powerful and visible influence on learning. Feedback occurs when students are cared for, interacted with, and patiently required to be mutually accountable for engaging in the learning process using their strengths as a scaffold to build upon.

Demystifying College: Undergraduate Foundations

Demystifying the college experience simply means ensuring that students understand what opportunities college can give them access to. Through this process, students also develop a better and more detailed understanding of what is at stake if they do not choose to continue their education beyond high school. As the Lopez brothers of the No Excuses network (King & Lopez, 2008) of schools explain, it is about creating a "culture of universal achievement" on your school campus and leading the charge for this crucial effort. This culture is developed so that every member of the staff believes that each child is capable of meeting standards in all content areas and that the school has the responsibility to make this opportunity a reality.

Leaders must ensure that staff members understand the power that they have to neutralize the many challenges that children shelve or bring with them when they come to school each day. Slogans of hope can be displayed throughout the school to motivate children and adults in their persistent journey to reach goals and experience a

Figure 2.3

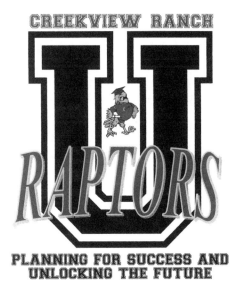

CREEKVIEW RANCH

RAPTORS

PLANNING FOR SUCCESS AND UNLOCKING THE FUTURE

promising future. These slogans can include such phrases as "Work Hard, Be Kind," "No Shortcuts," "Take Responsibility," "Own It!," "Knowledge Is Power," "All of Us Will Learn," and "Dedication, Desire, and Discipline."

Some staff members have often asked me why this is so important. What is at stake? Some staggering statistics from the U.S. Census Bureau (2009) bring the brutal facts about high school dropouts to light. Young adults who fail to complete high school earn approximately $16,485 a year and are 15 percent less likely to be employed when compared to high school graduates. Seventy-five percent of state prison inmates did not finish high school. On a more serious note, graduating from high school can be a matter of life or death as high school graduates have a greater life expectancy. In fact, they live an average of 9 years longer than dropouts and have improved decision-making abilities, higher incomes, safer work environments, and more access to important resources such as health insurance.

When leading the charge to demystify college for your staff and students, it is important to explain that college does not have to mean that all students attend school at a 4-year institution. A college experience will be different for students depending on many factors such as access and their skill base. Students must also equate college with junior colleges and trade schools such as cosmetology schools and medical technician certifications. The key point to drive home is that college means extending education beyond high school. Students respond well to numbers and statistics because they help them to set higher expectations for themselves. The following statistics about income and its relationship to college degree completion will motivate students to dream big and work harder:

- Trade school or an associate degree will allow students to earn approximately $37,492 annually.
- A bachelor's degree results in an average income of $50,024.
- A master's degree earns students slightly more at $51,509.
- A doctoral degree results in approximately $70,165 annually.

(U.S. Census Bureau, 2009)

Leaders need to create a culture of college readiness in their schools so students have clearer targets to aim for and can begin envisioning their futures early in their school careers. *College readiness* can be defined as an idea that all students deserve the opportunity to be educated in a way that prepares them for college should they choose to attend. Other ways students can become college ready is by exposing them to university requirements, high school A–G requirements, and college vocabulary such as diploma, degree, graduate, dormitory, and undergraduate (see Appendix B). Trips to local colleges and universities can open up a whole new landscape of opportunities for students, many of whom may have not had any immediate family members who have attended college. If field trips are not cost effective, most alumni associations are easy to contact and will send a local graduate to share information about higher education to your students. Another type of visitor who can inspire students because of his or her age would be a recent graduate from the neighborhood high school. These recent graduates will discuss life after high school and can stress the importance of working hard while in school.

A leader's role in creating a college-ready culture to improve student learning is about action and focus. Effective leaders prepare their staff to embark on a journey of continuous improvement with a laser-like focus on being an exceptional system driven by results. When creating this system, all stakeholders in the school should consistently seek out unique solutions to problems, collaborate in a student-centered way, and effectively develop consensus before making decisions that impact the entire school system or its students.

Protective Possibilities

When considering the context of the entire school, protective possibilities can be formed more globally as well. Extracurricular activities and leadership opportunities foster a sense of community and create buy-in toward a school experience (Benard, 2004, p. 166). Peer conflict management programs focus on the essential skill of problem solving and foster positive and long-lasting peer relationships. Consistent and well-publicized standards for behavior (see Appendix F) create "clear and consistent boundaries and logical consequences" and strengthen student autonomy (p. 166).

Students should be taught two to three basic overarching school rules. They must also be explicitly taught what it looks like to follow and break these rules throughout all areas of the campus. For example, if the rule is "Be Safe" then students must be able to differentiate between what being safe looks like in the multipurpose or lunch room versus on the basketball court or in the science lab. These standards for behavior must be enlarged on posters placed in every classroom and common area on a school site. Students must see the behavior standards wherever they are at school. They can then visualize daily what the rules are and what they should specifically do to keep from breaking them.

Staff members can participate in a powerful process of sorting their current student list by their needed level of support and their risk factors (see Appendix L). Some of these factors may include attendance, behavior, academics, health, and family dynamics or involvement. Each risk factor can be given a scale from one to three. A one indicates that the student has a low level of risk for that specific factor. A three is equated with a great deal of risk. Scores are tabulated, and students with the highest score are identified as extremely at risk and in need of urgent intervention. The teachers are now armed with this data and ready to make informed decisions about their response to the levels of risk in their schools. They work with the entire school system and families to mobilize resources and differentiate for student needs, which may be of an academic, social, or emotional nature. Once the resources are identified and secured, a growth plan is developed to address the areas of greatest need and to help students overcome challenges and risk factors.

Structural Elements

When seeking to foster a positive climate for learning, school structural elements are key. Displays of student work, student government, student jobs, frequent homework, and high rates of teacher-to-student interactions are all associated with improvements in school behavior (Embry, 1997, p. 5). Playground games that are organized reduce aggression. A common language should be shared between staff members and students about how to reach to new heights and improve learning outcomes. Other structural elements that have been found to be successful are notes of praise, posters about positive behavior, social skills lessons, and procedures and routines for common use areas (p. 9).

Resiliency is about cementing connections, building relationships, and developing a solid web of support for the needs of all students, whatever it takes. Actions take the place of excuses and blame in school settings where all students are protected and nurtured. Students learn in these settings not under the direction of a teacher but through the targeted facilitation of coordinated adult interventions from all stakeholders. When students come to school without the desire to learn and excel, we can accept their lack of motivation as is and carry on as we have year after year. However, I passionately feel that a very different type of action is our moral and ethical obligation to "help them overcome even the worst of life circumstances to compete every day in school" (Riley, 2006, p. 2).

The choice is simple and urgent, because it involves our most precious commodity, children. Despite their family dynamics or economic disadvantages, all children deserve nothing less than our best. The aforementioned schoolwide systems and strategies that are supported by decades of resiliency research will help educators fulfill the necessary commitment of learning for all students. They will also assist schools in closing achievement gaps that persist in our current deficit-driven system.

3 The Engaging Classroom Team

The Classroom Game Plan

PERSPECTIVES ON ENGAGEMENT

Research reviewed in previous chapters along with focused student data have demonstrated the power engaging classrooms can have on student learning. Both of these protective factors are essential when building resiliency. More on the student voices later in this book. Downey (2008) made some critical recommendations for classroom teachers to increase opportunities for meaningful student participation. Students must understand how academic content relates to their lives. This learning purpose can then be related to each student's academic and future goals.

Students are engaged when they are encouraged to contribute to classroom rules, routines, and schedules. Students need to have input for daily classroom activities to develop a sense of belonging and ownership. Cooperative learning can also assist students in becoming personally responsible for classroom contributions. Downey concludes her recommendations for fostering student engagement with suggested strategies for developing "transferable life skills" (p. 61). These skills should include interpersonal and communication skills, extracurricular activities, and literacy skill development. Extracurricular activities allow students to use their time before or after school in a positive manner and gain a broad range of experiences in the school community. Interactions in the classroom during peer-learning activities and between adults and students can be magical and a source of strength for at-risk students. "Educational resilience" can be experienced when students have supportive chances to cope with stress, manage conflict, problem solve, think critically, and make important decisions about their learning (p. 61).

Engaging Classrooms: Solutions for Student Success

Bonnie Benard (2004) provides specific examples of how classroom teachers and support staff can more effectively engage students. These classroom levels of support are listed in Table 3.1 and can be implemented most effectively by focusing on improving instruction and support structures one step at a time. Staff members should have input on where to begin improvement efforts, but most of these decisions are driven by each school's current reality and the needs of the students. Engagement also involves giving students a voice, which will be addressed in an upcoming chapter.

Getting in the Game:

Students must be cared for by the adults in their schools. Simultaneously, they also need to be required to get in the game and learn through meaningful participation.

Students must be able to make choices in the classroom, be active problem solvers, use imagination and creativity to construct meaning, and work collaboratively with their peers daily as they process essential learnings (p. 79). One example of how teachers can effectively tap into each student's creativity is a hero/heroine short story project (see Appendix M). Students reflect on the qualities and high moral and ethical values of a hero/heroine. They then identify some people in their lives or in popular media who possess these qualities. Students are allowed to give their heroes/heroines strengths or super powers that benefit society, but they must simultaneously note their weaknesses. Stories about the heroes/heroines are then developed, and illustrations accompany the story in a comic book format.

Through this project, students have been required to use their creative strengths, identify heroic attributes of people, and develop a story about a hero they wish to create. All these elements together empower them to work harder in school and in life. The project sends each student clear messages about what life skills he or she should strive to develop. This project illustrates that when students are active participants in their own learning they are able to meet a fundamental need for power and autonomy (p. 80).

Table 3.1

The Game Plan: The Engaging Classroom

An engaging classroom has the following elements in place or under construction:

❏ Cooperative groups abound and students work with learning partners during guided instruction and independent practice.

❏ Learning is connected to the real world as well as student strengths and interests.

❏ Students have opportunities to plan, make decisions, and problem solve throughout the school day.

❏ Class meetings are held regularly to celebrate small and big wins, focus on life skills, and solve peer issues and conflicts.

❏ Creative expression occurs through multiple mediums (art, music, writing, drama).

❏ Students are consistently asked to describe and use their strengths, goals, and dreams for academic success and peer support.

❏ Classroom goals allow students to unite in a common focus and work together to reach their objectives (see Appendix G for example).

❏ Peers are a primary source of support, including tutoring and mentoring.

❏ Students are involved in school-improvement efforts.

❏ Students are involved in service-learning projects.

❏ Students are given time every 15 to 20 minutes to stand up for physical movement (as little as 30 seconds increases blood flow to the brain and jump-starts thinking and the processing of information).

❏ Students use whiteboards during guided practice to demonstrate understanding.

❏ Students are held mutually accountable for responding in the classroom (no hand raising!).

❏ During cooperative learning, every student has a specific role and responsibility to create a collaborative finished product (no sitting on the sideline!).

❏ Students work in both heterogeneous and homogeneous groups.

❏ Every 2 to 3 minutes, students briefly interact in pairs or small groups to process information.

Source: Adapted from Weinstein (1991).

PRACTICAL APPLICATIONS

Applying Benard's examples to increase engagement is most effective when teams of teachers implement the strategies across entire grade levels or systems of support. Every student deserves the right to be an essential contributor to classroom learning. He or she needs to do the learning instead of just hearing about it and passively receiving the content.

The following are practical and effective ways to raise the level of engagement in classrooms. Students are our greatest resource, and they are why we are in the business of education. By focusing on their need to drive the learning process, educators facilitate success like the conductor of an orchestra rather than telling students about the content in the form of lectures or what has been disguised as direct instruction.

Short-Term Goal Setting

At our middle school, we identified the most at-risk students by analyzing discipline and attendance data along with academic screening data. These students were disengaged, intentionally failing, and/or disrupting learning environments for other students. They needed to reconnect to the purpose of school and have some mentoring and guidance to reach their goals. However, these goals needed to be short-term so they could experience some short-term wins. Adults used a targeted full-court press as students met with administrators, teachers, and counselors to discuss the importance of setting goals and to define success.

> *The reason most people never reach their goals is that they don't define them or ever seriously consider them as believable or achievable. Winners can tell you where they are going, what they plan to do along the way, and who will be sharing the adventure with them.*
>
> —Denis Watley

Then students set academic or behavioral goals for 3 weeks into the future. Students who met their goals were publicly recognized and participated in a surprise team-building field trip to the local bowling alley (see Appendices J and E).

In setting short-term goals with students, it is essential to have students identify their personal and academic strengths that will support them in reaching their goals. They also must identify challenges or road blocks to success and come to terms with them. Before long, students all across campus were requesting to set goals with our staff. Therefore, we implemented Plans for Success in our advisory classes where every student self-monitored his or her academic performance each week and set short-term 6-week goals for success. Administration then rewarded students who reached their goals. The Plans for Success also included areas for student reflections and journaling as well as templates for setting goals and planning for life beyond high school.

Dreamboards: Engaging in Future Success

This meaningful idea was brought to life by Oprah Winfrey in one of her thought-provoking episodes about her Angel Network. Dreamboards are visual representations of each student's future and engage students in visualizing their present and future successes in academic settings and in life. To keep costs to a minimum, schools ask parents and staff members to bring in school-appropriate magazines. Each student maps out his or her future on a Dreamboard template (see Appendix H). Students then go through the magazines and create a display board with images and explanations of the college they would like to attend, their career aspirations, where they will live, and how they will get from point A to point B. At the center of each board, a graduation cap is purposefully placed on the top of each student's school photo. Every student proudly displays the visionary board in his or her home and school and revisits it often to dream big and feed aspirations to make those dreams a reality.

Our elementary students displayed their Dreamboards in the multipurpose room for a gallery walk that created hopeful pride for our most at-risk children and for staff, parents, and community members. As a result, each student's self-esteem and classroom participation was positively impacted. Students who created this impressive landscape of their future set more goals for themselves in each of their subject areas and were more likely to experience spikes in academic achievement. The following example of a Dreamboard template (Figure 3.1) is from Amanda who is a fourth grader.

As Amanda began to map out her future, her explanations became more detailed, and she started to eagerly ask questions so that she

Figure 3.1

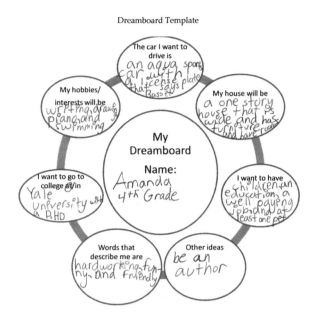

Dreamboard Template

could accurately capture her vision. For example, she learned about Yale University from a masterful third-grade teacher. This teacher wrote to Yale who then informally adopted the classroom and its students. The students wore Yale colors on Wednesdays, received care packages from alumni associations, and learned a great deal about its rich history. However, Amanda was not sure what type of degree she would have after attending Yale. After hearing about bachelor's, master's, and doctoral degrees, she decided to aim for the stars and noted that a PhD was in her future. As evident in this example, when students are asked to fill in the graphic organizer, they begin to tenaciously seek out more information about careers, hobbies, places to raise a family, automobiles, and colleges or universities.

Reading Rocks

Engaging students in daily reading practice is crucial for vocabulary development, reading fluency, creativity, comprehension, and the list goes on and on. However, many at-risk students disengage from this practice because they do not have books in their homes, their parents do not read, or because English is not their primary language. To support these students and require this crucial practice, we used multiple sources of reading assessment data to identify students in need of the most intensive reading support. We then asked students who were two or more grade levels above these students to be reading mentors. These mentors were recommended by their teachers because they were confident readers who were open to building caring relationships with younger students.

Reading Rocks came on the scene shortly thereafter, because the older students felt that we needed a theme to keep the after-school reading in the library fun and so that students would come back each day. A small budget for inflatable guitars, a Mohawk wig (the teacher's idea!), old records, and cutouts of musical notes can transform a reading nook in the library to a rockin' scene. The mentors can bring in rock music that can be screened by the supervising teacher. There was some harmonious magic created in that library nook as students found pleasure in simply reading with a newfound friend in an environment that was kid friendly, meaningful, and safe.

But how did this mentoring program impact the students? Students rocked their reading assessments, improved their reading levels, and checked more books out of the library to take home on a weekly basis. The at-risk students benefited from the practice and support of their mentors. At the same time, the older students learned how to build caring relationships, work as a team, and support schoolmates in a purposeful way. This program received many requests for an encore and maintains its fidelity and powerful practices after years of implementation.

College Readiness: Graduate-Level Applications

Students in elementary and middle schools tend to focus on the present because they are just beginning to discover who they are and what they can become. However, understanding a bit about the future that lies ahead of them is paramount for higher graduation rates, college attendance, and for them to be competitive on a local or global scale. College symbolism on our campus was a terrific way to for our students to dream big and realize the importance of being college ready.

Each teacher sent a letter to the alumni association of a favorite college or university as well as the university itself. Teachers received everything from banners to posters, pennants, and brochures on their adopted institutions of higher learning. Each class designed a poster representing their college or university that was displayed in the multipurpose room and house flags were purchased for each classroom to fly outside the door on Flag Fridays. Students were encouraged to wear college colors on Fridays and at school events. School spirit improved and activities such as a college fight song challenge motivated them to support their colleges or universities in a positive and vocal way. Students who performed their school's fight song for administration received a simple treat such as Popsicles or fruit snacks. Some students even used their band instruments for the performances and props. A local university was so impressed that they sent their marching band to play at the school's annual Jog-A-Thon. Go Aggies!

Not all students may attend college, but it is our responsibility to prepare them and get them academically fortified in case they make that choice beyond high school. Part of this preparation must include the demystification of college or university life as well as their requirements, resources, and options. Without a clear vision of what they can achieve beyond high school, many at-risk students get trapped in their cycles of poverty, closed doors, and broken dreams. Their parents' lower education levels become a self-fulfilling prophecy. Schools must make college readiness a priority to successfully prepare their students for brighter futures and diverse career options and to give them the hope they need to rise above risk and adversity.

Cost-Effective Whiteboards: Every Learner Plays the Game

Effective lesson design has a direct instruction component followed by guided and independent practices. During most guided practice sessions, students are asked to do a number of problems or activities on worksheets or handouts before teachers check for understanding. An alternative to these drill and kill pages is to use cost-effective whiteboards (Figure 3.2). These boards give teachers more timely feedback during this practice so that they can adjust their instruction and effectively plan targeted interventions.

The idea for the whiteboards came from Gene, a visiting consultant who was working on strengthening instruction at our school. These whiteboards are consumable and consist of the following: a plastic sheet protector, a small square of black felt, a dry erase pen, and a colored card stock paper insert for the sheet protector. Often parents or community groups can be asked to donate these supplies.

As teachers gradually release responsibility, students are asked to get out their whiteboards to write down the steps to a problem, a word, an answer, or a graphic representation or organizer. Then they hold up their boards so the teacher can do a quick scan and check for understanding to identify who needs some small-group support during the independent practice phase of the lesson.

Figure 3.2

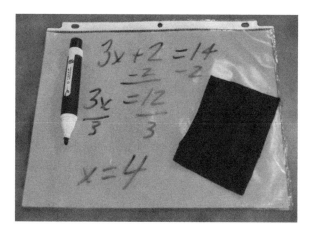

The colored card stock is important because without divulging it to the students, the teacher can target specific students or groups of students by assigning them a particular color for their insert. For example, if he or she just taught the class how to solve an equation in math, the students who did poorly on the last formative quiz or test can all be given orange sheets while others have green, blue, or another color. If the orange students are with the teacher and grasping how to solve the equation, the teacher can then check on the group that tends to perform on an average level on most math concepts. If 80% or more of these two groups of students are on target with solving the equations, this provides a good indication that the direct instruction was effective. The teacher can then gradually release even more responsibility until the students are successfully solving equations independently. This low-cost method of checking for understanding gets each and every student on the court at the same time. Like players, the students then try out by showing they are proficient at a particular skill.

Hands-Free Accountability

In classrooms all over the country, students are asked questions every few minutes. What happens next has been ingrained in our educational cultures to be acceptable. Students raise their hands. This seems to be the correct response, but we must ask ourselves who is raising their hands? Better yet, what about the students who are not?

Hand raising has its place in the classroom, but to guarantee that all students are mutually accountable to respond to teacher inquiries, an alternative must be implemented. Hands-free accountability involves writing the name of each student on a Popsicle stick or note card. As the teacher asks a question, sticks or cards are pulled and the student on the stick or card is asked to respond. Why is this effective? The answer is simple yet rarely practiced. Every child has an equal chance of being asked to get in the game so more students are engaged, listening, taking notes, and ready to play.

As teachers become more proficient at doing away with the ever-popular hand-raising phenomenon in their classrooms, they can experiment with additional strategies during this process. Cards can be shuffled every few days so that students cannot predict when their turn will come. At-risk students and those students who rarely participate can be given extra sticks or cards in the pile so they must respond more frequently to teacher questions. But what happens when a student is called on and has no response or answer? The teacher pulls another stick or card until the answer is given correctly by a student. The teacher then returns to the student who did not know the answer and asks them to repeat or paraphrase the correct answer that was shared by a peer. This rehearsal of the correct response is crucial because it ensures that when students are incorrect, they quickly practice the correct response in a risk-free setting.

This level of accountability is very basic if you just consider it at face value. However, applying these strategies on a daily basis will get all students in the game playing as a team as they support each other in responding to a school's instructional demands. Unfortunately, these practices are not implemented in most classrooms, because it has been ingrained in our pedagogical brains that students who want to share must raise their hands. Outlawing hand raising is liberating for both students and teachers. Educators can design and run the plays they want to use, and all players get equal playing time whether they are in the starting lineup or on the third string.

Engaging students in the classroom involves connecting them to what they are learning. We must require them to be active participants as they respond to instruction and process information. Achieving these goals means that the classroom teacher has to share the ball with students as they make their way to improved teamwork and academic outcomes. The remainder of this book will empower school and district leaders and teachers as it describes how to take a stand for student-centered practices. The rest of the game plan also involves giving students a voice and hearing from them about what caring relationships and engaged learning really mean to them. Finally, readers will be challenged to urgently and tenaciously initiate systemic change to narrow achievement gaps in their schools.

4

What We Urgently Stand For and Against

Does Your School Truly Put Student Learning First?

Every school would like to say that their mission is truly driven by student-centered practices. In fact, many mission and vision statements note student centeredness as the cornerstone of who they are and what they do. However, teacher-centered perspectives and other systemic roadblocks often get in the way of truly closing achievement gaps and improving student learning universally.

DuFour, DuFour, Eaker, and Many (2006) describe cultural shifts that must occur for a renewed focus on student learning to be realized (pp. 187–189). All stakeholders should become interdependent and move from identifying problems to strategically planning targeted solutions (p. 189). One fundamental shift is moving from covering all the content to having students demonstrate proficiency on essential content. Teachers move from focusing on what they taught to a relentless pursuit of ensuring that at least 80 percent of the students learned the content. In student-centered schools, interventions are required during the school day and are fluid based on frequent formative and common assessments. Another fundamental shift occurs when teachers do not allow the district or publisher pacing guides dictate their lesson planning and delivery. Instead, they ensure that the majority of students have mastered essential standards. It is then that they pick up the pace to move to the next fundamental skill.

Teachers do not go into classrooms thinking about all the ways that they will stay less focused on the students and more focused on what they require to get through their days. But teachers are faced will dwindling resources, archaic instructional models that they are asked to follow, and a plethora of other challenges. So what will help them turn the corner and experience a renewed laser like focus on student learning? Administrators must support them in the classroom while providing the catalyst for change, which includes the needed resources, state-of-the-art and research-driven staff development, the relentless pursuit of improved academic outcomes, and the accountable conversations that are necessary for schools to truly put student learning first.

TEACHER- VERSUS LEARNER-CENTERED PRACTICES

When assessing the student centeredness of their schools, leaders must truly understand the differences between teacher- and student-centered elements of support. Salinas and Garr (2009) effectively studied learner-centered schools and found that these schools had the following practices in common: project-based learning for students with choice, frequent formative feedback to students, encouragement of risk taking, and increasing student responsibility to facilitate their own learning. In addition, these practices were shown to increase student achievement especially for minority students (p. 229).

Relationships are key to student success. In his meta-analysis of learner-centered practices, Cornelius-White (2007) reviewed approximately 1,000 articles to "synthesize 119 studies. . . with 1,450 findings and 355,325 students" (p. 113). To say a study of this nature is comprehensive is an understatement. Cornelius-White uncovered many teacher behaviors and practices that improved student outcomes. Some of these included teachers encouraging creative and critical thinking, focusing on practices that increase student engagement, and avoiding "power struggles" by being empathetic to students' emotional and learning needs (p. 131). Positive relationships with students led to improved academic achievement in many studies as did creating classroom environments that fostered warmth and boosted self-esteem. In summary, student learning improved across numerous studies when teachers valued who students are, capitalized on their strengths, and facilitated classrooms where students were encouraged to take risks and dream big.

As school leaders, there are specific game plans that will result in teachers implementing more student-centered instructional practices. The first strategy involves doing quick classroom walk-throughs to collect data on the percentage of teacher talk that takes place during a 10-minute block of time. Armed with a campus map, stopwatch, and notepad, a school leader should spend no less than 10 minutes in every classroom. During that time, a stopwatch should be started and stopped every time a teacher begins and ends talking to his or her class. Ideally, the teacher-to-student ratio of communication should be approximately 5 minutes to 2 minutes.

> **Tenacious Caring:**
>
> In critical cases, caring adults must move beyond the aforementioned simple acts of caring to reach the most at-risk intentional nonlearners or those students who try harder to fail than they do to improve. This shift involves caring with tenacity or working harder at student success than students are working at failure.

The primary job of the teacher is to instruct on essential content and model. In actuality, the sit-and-get model that exists in most classrooms results in disengaged students who do not learn at high levels. When students are given time to talk with each other in pairs or small groups, it should be counted as student talk. This data should be averaged across all classrooms so teachers feel safe discussing the data and looking at schoolwide patterns. The resulting data will most likely be an eye-opener to the majority of administrators who collect it. Other data that can be collected to assess the student centeredness of a school and its classrooms is the amount of time students spend working alone versus working collaboratively with their peers.

Another crucial element of a student-centered school and classroom is the amount of time students are given to evaluate their own learning along with the teacher. When students are consistently asked to self-assess their academic performance, progress toward goals, behavior, participation, or attendance, they are more likely to self-correct and improve their academic achievement. According to famed researcher Hattie (2009) and his meta-analyses of what positively impacts student learning, students' self-assessments of their progress and outcomes have the largest impact on student achievement. Quick formative evaluations allow students to see their mistakes and disaggregate their causes. Additionally, students who are required to carefully review their mistakes for patterns are less likely to repeat similar missteps in the future.

Student-centered classrooms are not quiet. There is a lot of productive noise with students questioning, interacting, and spending time on task working toward mastery of learning objectives.

Unfortunately, too many classrooms house students who must sit and listen for minutes and hours on end. Students in these environments learn very little and disengage at a rapid pace.

CREATING A SENSE OF URGENCY

Administrators can do a great deal to require student-centered practices in their schools, but first they must create the urgency for teachers to change their daily classroom practices. Numbers typically paint the most accurate picture for teachers about their students. More specifically, proficiency scores from local or state tests over time make the most lasting impact. Each subgroup's percentage of proficiency that is tracked over a minimum of 4 years can be displayed on a common line graph. This type of graph is the most effective way to visually expose achievement gaps between subgroups. Then challenging and reflective questions can be asked of educators to push them to conclude that some or many large groups of students in their schools are not learning.

FACES OF THE ACHIEVEMENT GAP

This graph opens up the conversation and dialogue, but it is the faces of the students themselves that paints the most urgent and realistic picture. For a staff meeting or staff development meeting, administrators can print pictures of the students by grade level who have scored below proficient on a current common assessment. These pictures have no student information on them except the student's first and last name. After these pictures are posted, a red line is drawn next to the photos, and to the right of the line, the pictures of the proficient students are posted. Teachers can then be asked to write in journals about the data, select specific students to mentor and develop action plans on, or collect all the photos of the nonproficient students for a grade level and have powerful collaborative conversations about what is getting in the way of learning essential content for these students.

OWN IT!

Accepting responsibility for educating the nonproficient students is challenging. Educators do not go into their classrooms each day to make sure students do not learn. On the contrary, they work themselves to the bone trying to launch student achievement to new heights. Admitting there are students who require intensive care takes honesty and courage. Teachers must be asked to "own it" or take on the responsibility of doing something to change the academic trajectories of the low-performing subgroups in their schools. Owning it is not about placing blame on others, each child's parents, or their difficult upbringing. Owning it means realizing that there is a lot that teachers cannot control or influence. However, teachers must also realize that they harness incredible powers to intervene with students and allow them to rebound from risk and adversity. Owning it means truly understanding that in many cases, a teacher is often the only consistent adult in a child's life who can help them experience a turning point. Owning it also means committing to implementing what works in schools such as the aforementioned student-centered practices. The classroom and school practices mentioned in previous chapters in this book are just some of the ways that teachers can formulate a successful game plan to level the playing field. Nonproficient students from at-risk subgroups benefit greatly from this renewed focus. By using this book's strategies, tools, and templates, educators will foster caring adult–student relationships and will improve student engagement across school campuses.

5 All-Star Performance

What Will Your Legacy Be?

The Leadership Implications
of Systemic Change for All Students

TRANSFORMATIONAL LEADERS AS AGENTS OF CHANGE

The strategies, tools, and ideas in this book have implications for transformational leaders who seek to strengthen staff members' collective capacity to positively change students' outcomes. Leaders who transform give all stakeholders in their organization a voice including the students. Initiating change without student voices, which must be heard through surveys, interviews, or informal conversations, leaves out critical pieces of the transformative puzzle. Transformational leaders should attempt to raise the levels of personal commitments from their organizational members and in the name of social justice should strategically keep formidable forces of resistance at bay (Theoharis, 2007, p. 248). These commitments are the organization's goals for student success.

Fostering resiliency can improve student outcomes as demonstrated by years and years of research and practice. These amazing levels of academic growth create the motivation that is needed for staff members to feel and act on the sense of urgency for organizational and pedagogical changes. Leaders who require educators to develop caring and engaging relationships with all students will improve student learning. Leithwood and Jantzi (2006) found that leadership in a school has an influence on whether or not teachers change their instructional practices (p. 223). More important, "the potency of leadership for increasing student learning hinges on the specific classroom practices which leaders stimulate, encourage, and promote" (p. 223).

OWN THE CHALLENGE

Leaders who effectively advance social justice in their schools have knowledge and skills in special education and in working with English learners. They also possess a deep and compassionate understanding of the issues surrounding race and poverty, and these leaders excel when working with families from diverse backgrounds (Theoharis, 2007, p. 250). Leaders themselves must develop resiliency as they hit road blocks to social justice head-on. They may do this through "enhancing reflective consciousness and developing a broader knowledge and skills base" (Theoharis, 2007, p. 250).

Leadership Applications: Practices for Transformation and Justice

Exercising leadership that truly transforms student learning will require collective strong commitments and leaders with a global perspective on issues such as social justice, equitable teaching practices, and inclusive education. Clarity is also needed about what systemic supports hold all stakeholders accountable for establishing caring adult–student relationships and facilitating student engagement. Mandates from the top down should be questioned by leaders if they do not promote effective instruction and improved student outcomes. Glanz (2007) called for courageous leadership where leaders "stand up despite opposition" to changes and initiatives that conflict with what studies and research have shown is in the best interest of teachers and students (p. 128). According to Glanz, without courage leaders "become mere technicians, administrative guardians, nothing more than custodians of the institution" (p. 129).

Relentless and Accountable Caring

Disenfranchised students need school administrators who adamantly pursue the highest level of caring and engagement for them every minute of every instructional day. Transformational leadership is being daring and driven enough to confront difficult and uncomfortable situations in the best interest of supporting all students, whatever it takes. Transformational leaders have charisma, want to influence others, and have strong moral values (Glanz, 2007, p. 130).

Fullan (2003) developed five critical mind-sets and actions that leaders "must cultivate: a deep sense of moral purpose, knowledge of the change process, capacity to develop relationships across diverse individuals and groups, skills in fostering knowledge creation and sharing, and the ability to engage with others in coherence amidst multiple innovations" (p. 35). When cultivating resiliency in their schools, school leaders should zero in on the action of building relationships with staff members and on requiring them to demonstrate caring with all students. Resiliency also relies on leaders to hold teachers accountable for engaging their students. Leaders must also encourage them to become classroom innovators and provide them with the necessary resources and tools.

THE SOUL OF A LEADER

In the words of Bolman and Deal (1995) and their book *Leading With Soul*, "leading is giving. Leadership is an ethic, a gift of oneself. It is easy to miss the depth and power of this message" (p. 102). According to Bolman and Deal, leadership is not merely visions of excellence or positive change. It is the "gift of self" that becomes reciprocal the more it is set into action (p. 102). The gift of love is also essential for leading with soul, which these authors define as a willingness to be caring, vulnerable, and respectful. The gift of power engages others in working toward a common goal or cause and possibly disempowering oneself as the leader to raise the influence of others. The final gift of significance serves leaders well, because it provides "a coherent sense of meaning" (p. 109). As Bolman and Deal (1995) so poetically state, "when ritual and ceremony are authentic and attuned, they fire the imagination, evoke insight, and touch the heart" (p. 111). The affect of the heart and the ethic of caring are essential for leaders to embrace and develop if they truly feel the urgency to narrow achievement gaps for their disenfranchised students.

> **Let Their Voices Be Heard:**
>
> In *Caring as Tenacity* (2000), Pitman and Zorn state that adults must persist by ensuring that school is a safe environment for students where they can take risks and be heard. Students must establish positive relationships with multiple adults on school campuses who appreciate who they are and are "encouraged to be who they might dare to become" (p. 93). Tenacious caring occurs when adults truly commit to students, set realistic expectations, and learn about students' lives outside of school.

CONCLUSION

We all remember teachers who touched our lives. These teachers cared about us, had high expectations for our success, and engaged us actively in the learning process every minute of every instructional day. They respected our uniqueness, talents, and interests. We were visible while students in other classrooms were invisible and left behind.

History books and memoires are full of examples of caring teachers who have touched the lives of their students. Anne Sullivan believed that Helen Keller could read and write even though she was deaf and blind (Lumpkin, 2007, p. 158). Jaime Escalante helped students of poverty in East Los Angeles achieve remarkable levels of success in math because he "refused to accept the prevailing attitude that these youth could not overcome past educational deprivations" (p. 158).

I passionately feel that being a transformational teacher and leader requires a different type of engagement. Educators, leaders, and policymakers must be engaged in the continuous improvement of our schools and classrooms. This level of engagement means zero tolerance for achievement gaps. It means courageously requiring all who work with our youth to establish connections with and engage all students, especially those at risk of school failure or who have become polarized by risk and adversity. Teachers who engage their students in the learning process do so as conductors of active student involvement resulting in an orchestra of learning and success. Students are not only hearing and seeing learning happen, they are doing the learning with their peers while the teacher takes on the role of a facilitator. Actively involved students process new content by working with their peers through problem-based inquiries and real-world applications.

The protective factors of resiliency in the lives of vulnerable children increase the odds of those children overcoming adverse life experiences (Katz, 1997, p. 49). The talents of students who overcome high levels of risk are showcased and valued so they can develop a sense of mastery and success. Students become resilient and more academically successful when they feel that they really matter. Resilient students' contributions are seen as crucial to collectively understanding content objectives.

In facing life's challenges, there is no greater resource than schools for "protecting, nourishing, and stimulating children raised under conditions of severe adversity" (Katz, 1997, p. 96). Schools and the professionals within them have the often unharnessed power to nourish students' talents, intervene where students are vulnerable, enhance the interpersonal skills that are necessary for strong caring relationships to develop, and "permanently alter the developmental trajectories of children" (p. 96). Schools that offer greater protective possibilities have been shown to house higher levels of achievement than less protective schools whose students were exposed to the same environmental and societal risks.

I encourage you to hear the voices of the students and allow these voices to drive the improvement efforts at your school or in your school district. If we do not ask students what they need to be successful, how can we claim that we are effectively providing them with the essentials of learning? The answer is that we cannot be truly effective in responding to student needs without first caring about what students have to say about their experiences and needs.

TURNING POINTS

The protective factors of resiliency can provide turning-point experiences for the most at-risk student subgroups. Turning points occur when an environment and the people who work within it recognize a child's strengths and talents and therefore open up new opportunities for that child (Katz, 1997, p. 152). Children need leaders and educators who are driven by a sense of hope and are energized into action by the opportunity of turning-point experiences for their students. Conditions and circumstances of risk can be insurmountable for young children as they continually fail year after year. However, "new sources of protection, strength, and understanding" will propel them over treacherous mountains of adversity (p. 153). The protective possibilities of caring adult relationships and student engagement are those sources of protection that indeed make a difference in the academic outcomes of students. **I conclude this book with a call to action for educators, leaders, and policymakers. That action is the creation of turning points for all students despite their levels of risk.** Last, I have included a poem by Myra B. Welch (1993) that powerfully conveys the incredible hope and transformative power that can be generated by a master creating a turning point for a child (as cited in Katz, 1997, pp. 158–160).

> 'Twas battered and scarred, and the auctioneer
> Thought it scarcely worth his while
> To waste much time on the old violin,

But held it up with a smile.
'What am I bidden, good folks,' he cried.
'Who'll start the bidding for me?
A dollar, a dollar,' then, two! Only two?
'Two dollars, and who'll make it three?
Three dollars once; three dollars, twice;
Going for three —' But no,
From the room, far back, a grey-haired man
Came forward and picked up the bow;
Then, wiping the dust from the old violin,
And tightening the loose strings,
He played a melody pure and sweet
As a caroling angel sings.

The music ceased, and the auctioneer,
With a voice that was quiet and low,
Said: 'What am I bid for the old violin?'
And he held it up with the bow.
'A thousand dollars, and who'll make it two?
Two thousand! And who'll make it three?
Three thousand, once; three thousand, twice
And going and gone,' said he.
The people cheered, but some of them cried,
'We do not quite understand
What changed its worth?' Swift came the reply:
'The touch of a master's hand.'

And many a man with life out of tune,
And battered and scarred with sin,
Is auctioned cheap to the thoughtless crowd,
Much like the old violin.
A "mess of potage," glass of wine;
A game and he travels on.
He is "going" once, and "going" twice,
He's "going" and almost "gone."
But the Master comes and the foolish crowd
Never can quite understand
The worth of a soul and the change that's wrought
By the touch of the Master's hand.

The poem "The Touch of the Master's Hand," by Myra Brooks Welch was first published in the February 26, 1921 issue of *The Gospel Messenger* (now called the *Messenger*), later published by the Brethren Publishing House.

Appendix A

ENVISIONING LIFE BEYOND HIGH SCHOOL

ESSENTIAL ELEMENTS OF SUCCESS AT CRMS

- ☑ Check yourself: Weekly checks during advisory on your progress in all classes, attendance, and behavior
- ☑ Short-term goals every 6 weeks
- ☑ Rewards from administration/teachers for meeting those goals!
- ☑ Use your academic/personal strengths to achieve your goals
- ☑ Get ready for high school and beyond!

Get College Ready!

THE WORLD IS YOURS!

- Be prepared: Listen, study, show what you know
- Learn academic and social skills: knowledge is power
- Solve problems: create solutions
- Choose a path to success: be career oriented

You deserve these opportunities, so seize the day!

WHY SHOULD OUR STUDENTS THINK ABOUT HIGH SCHOOL AND GOING TO COLLEGE?

They will have greater career and promotion opportunities.

They will add greater value to our society.

They will have a higher quality of life.

They will have greater opportunities to pursue hobbies, personal interests, wealth, and stability.

WHAT IS COLLEGE READINESS?

The idea that every student deserves the opportunity to be educated in a way that prepares them for college if they so choose to attend.

WHO WILL PREPARE OUR STUDENTS FOR COLLEGE?

The students themselves, our staff, the students' parents and family members, and our community.

WHEN WILL OUR STUDENTS GRADUATE FROM COLLEGE?

GRADE LEVEL	COLLEGE GRADUATION YEAR
6th	2022
7th	2021
8th	2020

HOW DO I GET COLLEGE READY AT CREEKVIEW?

Get involved (activities and clubs)

Do the hard work (homework, class work, studying for tests)

Get extra help (if you need it)

Stay on a positive path (make great choices and use your life skills)

Appendix B

DEMYSTIFYING COLLEGE

COLLEGE READINESS VOCABULARY AND COLLEGE-LEVEL ACADEMIC WORDS BY GRADE LEVEL

Below are the words that each grade level has committed to using in their classes as we promote college readiness for all. Please work with your team to continuously expose students to the *college readiness vocabulary* and **college-level academic words** within your grade's column as well as all the grades before you.

College Readiness Vocabulary

Kindergarten	1st Grade	2nd Grade	3rd Grade	4th Grade	5th Grade
college	achieve	major	advisor	All words K–3	All words K–3
	career	mascot	alumni	Focus on A–G	Focus on A–G
	goal	professor	application	Get Ready for College curriculum	Get Ready for College curriculum

(Continued)

Continued

Kindergarten	1st Grade	2nd Grade	3rd Grade	4th Grade	5th Grade
	graduate	scholarship	bachelor's degree		
		dormitory	dean's list		
			finals		
			GPA		
			grants		
			loan		
			NCAA		
			research		

College-Level Academic Words by Grade Level

Kindergarten	1st Grade	2nd Grade	3rd Grade	4th Grade	5th Grade
area	available	analyze	assume	data	contract
approach	benefit	assess	authority	policy	define
create	consist	assume	concept	process	derive
estimate	distribute	context	constitute	research	interpret
	respond	role	indicate	section	issue
		similar	individual	significant	legal
			identify	specific	legislate
			proceed	structure	occur
				theory	period
				vary	principle

Appendix C

LIFE SKILLS

RAPTORS:
THE WORLD IS YOURS!

LIFE SKILLS WILL GET YOU COLLEGE READY:
USE THE KEYS TO SUCCESS

AUGUST
Initiative
I Make Decisions and Get Things Done

SEPTEMBER
Self-Control
I Use Common Sense

OCTOBER
Confidence
I Can and Will Do It

DECEMBER
Honesty
I Am Prepared

JANUARY
Reliability
You Can Count On Me

FEBRUARY
Cooperation
I Work Well with Others: I Contribute

MARCH
Team Spirit
I Sacrifice for Others

APRIL
Intentness
I Never Give Up on My Goals

MAY
Adaptability
I Make It Work No Matter What

Appendix D

ENRICHMENT OPPORTUNITIES

SUCCESS: Begins on 04/17/12

OPEN SESSIONS MENU

*If you have a room number next to your name on the roster, *you must* go to that room assignment.

For OPEN session students:

*If a session is full, please go to another open session

Success Class	Location
Run, Jog, Walk Club	Track
Study Hall/AR	D08
Jewelry Making (new jewelry makers only)	D05
6th grade Greek Mythology	D02
WEB (WEB leaders only)	D01
3D CAD Design	Tech Lab
Chess	F05
Create Your Own Super Hero (writing)	F07
AR Support	F03
Mime	F08
Tennis	Blacktop
AR Support	R03
Study Hall/SS Paper Rewrite	R04
Virtual PE	R06
Civil War Enrichment: Gettysburg	R07
Frontiers of Science II	D06
AR	D09
HW Center	F09
Indoor Games	D07
Book Club: Jurassic Park	F10

Appendix E

STUDENT GROWTH PLAN

Trimester One: Goal Planning Guide

This is my goal:

By _____ (date) I will _____

_____ (measure of improvement/score) by focusing on _____ (actions and skills).

My goal is important to me because _____

_____

I will reach my goal because I have the following strengths:

1. _____ 2. _____ 3. _____

I need to own that the following roadblocks are there but I can get around them:

1. _____ 2. _____ 3. _____

(Continued)

(Continued)

This is exactly what I am going to do to reach my goal. It is my action plan and to-do list:

☑ _____

☑ _____

☑ _____

I can count on these people to help me reach my goal: _____

This is how I will check how I am doing along the way: _____

This goal is important to me because _____

Student Academic Goal Sheet

Name: _____   2nd Grade End-of-Year Goal: 90+   3rd Grade End-of-Year Goal: 110+

Goal Area: **Reading Fluency** *(correct words per minute)*

January Actual Score	February Actual Score	March Actual Score	April Actual Score	Gain/Loss +/-

April Goal: _____

In order to reach my goal, I will:

1. _____
2. _____
3. _____

Student Signature: _____

Parent Signature: _____

Teacher Signature: _____

Appendix F

SCHOOLWIDE STANDARDS FOR BEHAVIOR

Behavior Expectations: ALL Areas of Campus

	Be Safe.	*Be Responsible.*	*Be Respectful.*
Universal (In All Areas)	• Keep hands, feet, and objects to yourself • Walk at all times • Remain in supervised or designated areas • Keep prohibited items at home • Use your life skills	• Clean up after yourself • Leave gum at home • Use cell phones in authorized areas • Be punctual • Come to school prepared and ready to learn • Use your life skills	• Use appropriate language and actions • Respect property, yours and others' • Follow staff directions immediately (the first time) • Use appropriate volume in conversation • Use your life skills
All Classrooms	• Keep hands, feet, and objects to yourself • Remain in supervised or designated areas • Keep prohibited items at home	• Clean up after yourself • Leave gum at home • Use cell phones in authorized areas • Follow the dress code • Be punctual • Come to class prepared and ready to learn • Stay organized	• Use appropriate language and actions • Respect property, yours and others' • Follow staff directions immediately (the first time) • Use appropriate volume when speaking • Speak during appropriate times

(Continued)

Continued

	Be Safe.	*Be Responsible.*	*Be Respectful.*
Eating Areas	• Remain properly seated at tables	• Keep electronics turned off and in backpacks • Place trash and recyclables in appropriate containers	• Hoods and hats off when indoors • Wait in line patiently
Gym	• Sit properly • Use equipment properly • No food, drinks, or gum in gym	• Show good sportsmanship • Return equipment to designated area	• Be a team player • Encourage others
Assemblies/ Special Events	• Sit quietly during presentation • Wait for dismissal instructions	• Focus on the presentation and the guest speaker(s)	• Listen responsibly • Listen respectfully • Be present • Participate appropriately
Technology Lab/ Library	• Use chairs and tables appropriately • Leave backpacks in a safe, secure area	• Return materials to proper places on time • Use Internet appropriately • Have ID ready to present • No food, drinks, or gum	• Print only what is needed
Hallways	• Stay on walkways	• Move to class on time • Report situations and conditions that need attention	• Treat others with respect
Office	• Use chairs and tables appropriately	• Obtain permission to use phone • No food, drinks, or gum	• State your purpose politely
Restrooms	• Keep water in sink • Wash hands	• Inform adults of vandalism	• Give people privacy
Bicycles, Scooters, Skateboards, Pedestrians	• Wear helmets • Walk equipment on campus	• Secure bicycles	• Stay clear of private property and roads
Bus Stop	• Remain alert to potential hazards	• Wait in line patiently	• Stay clear of private property

Bus	• Follow driver directions immediately • Remain seated	• Have bus ID (and Bus Activity Pass) ready to present • Keep area clean • Maintain possession of your belongings	• Use appropriate volume in conversation
Locker Rooms	• Refrain from horseplay and loitering	• Lock your lockers • Account for all your belongings • Once dressed, report to designated locations	• Give others privacy
Extracurricular Activities/ Events	• Ensure necessary transportation home promptly	• Obtain a Bus Activity Pass if needed from the adviser	• Positively represent our school

Source: Creekview Ranch Middle School 2011–2012 (Banan, A., Carter, A., Cecil, J., & Stanley, L., 2009)

Appendix G

CLASSROOM GOALS (FIFTH-GRADE EXAMPLE)

Bachelor of Mathematics

(Multiplication timed test mastered)

Master of Mathematics

(Division timed test mastered)

Doctorate of Mathematics

(Two-minute test with BOTH multiplication AND division mastered)

Source: Miss Charpentier's 5th Grade Site @ https://sites.google.com/site/misscharpentiers homepage/what-s-your-thought-/classroomgoals

Appendix H

DREAMBOARD TEMPLATE

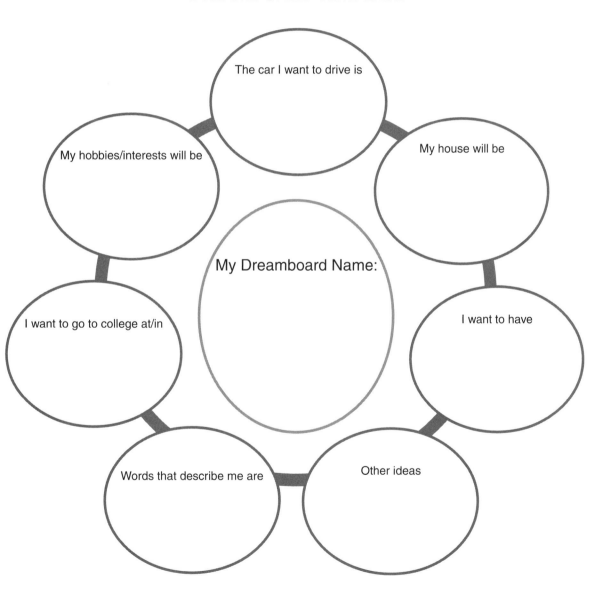

The car I want to drive is

My hobbies/interests will be

My house will be

My Dreamboard Name:

I want to go to college at/in

I want to have

Words that describe me are

Other ideas

Appendix I

HATTIE'S META-STRATEGIES FOR STUDENT GROWTH (2009)

Formative evaluation	0.9	
Classroom behavior (school structures)	0.8	
Teacher-to-student feedback	0.73	Large effect size
Teacher–student relationships	0.72	
Academic vocabulary	0.67	
Phonics interventions	0.6	
Study skills	0.59	
Reading comprehension programs	0.58	
Home environment	0.57	
SES	0.57	
Teacher goals	0.56	
Peer tutoring	0.55	
Classroom management (school structures)	0.52	
Parent involvement	0.51	Medium effect size
Small group	0.49	
Student engagement	0.48	
Math intervention	0.45	
Writing programs	0.44	
Teacher expectations	0.43	
Cooperative learning	0.41	
Social skills programs	0.4	

(Continued)

Continued

Enrichment	0.39	
Time on task	0.38	
Computer-assisted instruction	0.37	
School leaders	0.36	
Exposure to reading	0.36	
Drama/arts programs	0.35	
Teacher effects	0.32	
GATE ability grouping	0.3	
Homework	0.29	
Home visits	0.29	Small
Summer school	0.23	effect size
Teaching test taking	0.22	
Visual/audiovisual	0.22	
Class size	0.21	
Web-based learning	0.18	
Family structure	0.17	
Extracurricular programs	0.17	
Mentoring	0.15	
Ability grouping	0.12	
Combo classes	0.04	

Source: Adapted from Hattie, J. (2009) *Visible Learning.* New York: Routledge.

Appendix J

MY PLAN FOR SUCCESS

CRMS

Student's Name_____

Goal:

List something you would like to accomplish in the next 6 weeks.

_____

_____

_____

_____

_____

Help:

List qualities or characteristics you have that are strengths. These things will help you reach your goal (example: courage, social talent, independence, etc.).

☒ _____

☒ _____

☒ _____

☒ _____

Hang-Ups:

List qualities or characteristics about you that could stand in the way of you reaching your goal. (Example: angry sometimes, don't like to write, not good at math)

☒ _____

☒ _____

☒ _____

☒ _____

Strategies for achieving this goal:

Step to Take	When?	Who Can Help Me?

Appendix K

GRADE IMPROVEMENT PLAN

GPA at T1 Progress: _____

Days absent so far: _____

Current # behavior pts: _____

CREEKVIEW RANCH MIDDLE SCHOOL

Grade Improvement Plan

Student Name: _____

Date of Conference: _____

Focus Area(s): _____

What am I having the most difficulty with in this class?

What do I need to do to raise my grade?	*Who can help me?*	*Date*

What is the first step in achieving my goal of academic recovery?

_____   _____

Student Signature   Date

_____   _____

Parent Signature   Date

_____   _____

Counselor/Teacher/Administrator Signature   Date

Source: Adapted by Counselor Jillian Glende from *Enhancing RTI* (Fisher & Frey, 2010, ASCD).

Appendix L

LEVELS OF SUPPORT

Teacher Name: _____   Date: _____

*Please consider EVERYTHING you know about each of your current students and place <u>every child</u> in one of the support levels listed on the table below (see reverse for descriptors of each level).

Intensive Intervention and Support	Strategic Intervention and Support	Monitor and Support
1.	1.	1.
2.	2.	2.
3.	3.	3.
4.	4.	4.
5.	5.	5.
6.	6.	6.
7.	7.	7.

Intensive Intervention and Support	Strategic Intervention and Support	Monitor and Support
8.	8.	8.
9.	9.	9.
10.	10.	10.
11.	11.	11.
12.	12.	12.
13.	13.	13.
14.	14.	14.
15.	15.	15.
16.	16.	16.
17.	17.	17.
18.	18.	18.
19.	19.	19.
20.	20.	20.
21.	21.	21.
22.	22.	22.
23.	23.	23.

STRATEGIC INTERVENTION AND SUPPORT

Digging Deeper

Student Name	Academic Strengths	Academic Area(s) of Need	<u>Growth Plan:</u> (goals, benchmarks, interventions, assessments to address areas of need)

INTENSIVE INTERVENTION AND SUPPORT:

Digging Even Deeper

Student Name	Academic/ Social Strengths	Risk Inventory (Assign a 3 for significant impact on the child's learning, 2 for moderate impact, 1 for some impact)
*	*	Family background 1 2 3
	*	Parent support 1 2 3
	*	Health 1 2 3
	*	Attendance 1 2 3
	*	Academics 1 2 3
	*	Behavior 1 2 3
	*	**Detailed description of 3s, 2s, and 1s:**
	*	<u>Growth Plan</u> **(goals, benchmarks, interventions, assessments to address high-risk areas):**

References

Ainley, J. (1995). Students' views of their schools. *Unicorn, 21,* 5–16.

Anyon, Jean. *2005. Radical possibilities: Public policy, urban education, and a new social movement.* New York, NY: Routledge/Falmer.

Banan, A., Carter, A., Cecil, J., & Stanley, L. (2009). *Schoolwide standards for behavior.* Roseville, CA: Creekview Ranch Middle School BEST Team.

Battistich, V., & Hom, A. (1997). The relationship between students' sense of their school as a community and their involvement in problem behaviors. *American Journal of Public Health, 87,* 1997–2001.

Battistich, V., Watson, M., & Solomon, D. (1999). Beyond the three R's: A broader agenda for school reform. *Elementary School Journal, 99*(5), 415–432. Retrieved from Education Full Text database

Becker, B. E., & Luthar, S. S. (2002). Social-emotional factors affecting achievement outcomes among disadvantaged students: Closing the achievement gap. *Educational Psychologist, 37*(4), 197–214.

Benard, B. (1991). *Turning it around for all youth: From risk to resilience.* ERIC Clearinghouse on Urban Education. Retrieved from http://resilnet.uiuc.edu/library/dig126.html

Benard, B. (2004). *Resiliency: What we have learned.* San Francisco, CA: WestEd.

Bolman, L. G., & Deal, T. E. (1995). *Leading with soul.* San Francisco, CA: Jossey-Bass.

Brokenleg, M., & Bockern, S. V. (2003). The science of raising courageous kids. *Reclaiming Children and Youth, 12*(1), 22–27.

Burns, T. (1994) *From risk to resilience: A journey with heart for our future, our children.* Dallas, TX. Marco Polo Publishers.

Connell. J. P., & Wellborn, J. G. (1991). *Competence, autonomy, and relatedness: A motivational analysis of self-system processes.* In M. R. Gunnar & L. A. Sroufe (Eds.), Self processes in development: Minnesota Symposium on Child Psychology: Vol. 29 (pp. 244–254). Hillsdale, NJ: Lawrence Erlbaum.

Connor, C. M., Son, S.-H., Hindman, A. H., & Morrison, F. J. (2005). Teacher qualifications, classroom practices, family characteristics, and preschool experience: Complex effects on first graders' vocabulary and early reading outcomes. *Journal of School Psychology, 43,* 343–375.

Cornelius-White, J. (2007). Learner-centered teacher-student relationships are effective: A meta-analysis. *Review of Educational Research, 77*(1), 113–143.

Darling-Hammond, L. (2000). Greater expectations for student learning: The missing connections. *Liberal Education, 86*(2), 6–13. Retrieved from ERIC database

Deschenes, S., Cuban, L., & Tyack, D. (2001). Mismatch: Historical perspectives on schools and students who don't fit them. *Teachers College Record. 103*{4) 525-547.

Downey, J. A. (2008). Recommendations for fostering educational resilience in the classroom. *Preventing School Failure, 53*(7), 56–64.

DuFour, R., DuFour, R., Eaker, R., & Many, T. (2006). *Learning by doing: A handbook for professional learning communities at work.* Bloomington, IL: Solution Tree.

Embry, D. D. (1997). Does your school have a peaceful environment? Using an audit to create a climate for change and resiliency. *Intervention in School and Clinic, 32,* 217–222.

Entwisle, D. R., & Alexander, K. L. (1988). Factors affecting achievement test scores and marks of Black and White first graders. *Elementary School Journal, 88,* 449–471.

Fisher, D., & Frey, N. (2010). *Enhancing RTI: How to ensure success with effective classroom instruction and intervention.* ASCD.

Franco, B. (2000). *You hear me?* Cambridge, MA: Candlewick Press.

Fullan, M. (2003). Implementing change at the building level. In W. A. Owings & L. S. Kaplan (Eds.) *Best practices, best thinking, and emerging issues in school leadership.* Thousand Oaks, CA: Corwin.

Gándara, P. (2009). Progress and stagnation: 25 years of Hispanic achievement. *Diverse Issues in Higher Education, 26*(9), 37–38. Retrieved from Education Full Text database

Glanz, J. (2007). On vulnerability and transformative leadership: An imperative for leaders of supervision. *International Journal of Leadership in Education, 10*(2), 115–135.

Goodenow, C. (1993a). Classroom belonging among early adolescent students: Relationships to motivation and achievement. *Journal of Early Adolescence, 13,* 21–43.

Greenwood, C. R., Horton, B. T., & Utley, C. A. (2002). Academic engagement: Current perspectives on research and practice. *School Psychology Review, 31*(3), 328–349.

Hall, Q. (1997) as cited in Katz, M. (1997). *On playing a poor hand well.* New York, NY: W.W. Norton.

Hamre, B. K., & Pianta, R. C. (2001). Early teacher-child relationships and the trajectory of children's school outcomes through eighth grade. *Child Development, 72*(2), 625–638.

Hamre, B. K., & Pianta, R. C. (2005). Can instructional and emotional support in the first-grade classroom make a difference for children at risk of school failure? *Child Development, 76*(5), 949–967.

Hanson, T. L., & Austin, G. A. (2002). *Health risks, resilience, and the Academic Performance Index.* California Healthy Kids Survey Factsheet 1. Los Alamitos, CA: WestEd.

Hanson, T. L., Austin, G., & Lee-Bayha, J. (2004). *How are student health risks & resilience related to the academic progress of schools?* San Francisco, CA: WestEd.

Hargreaves, A., Earl, L., & Ryan, J. (1996). *Schooling for change: Reinventing education for early adolescents.* Washington, DC: Falmer Press.

Hattie, J. A. C. (2009). *Visible learning.* New York, NY: Routledge.

Hughes, J. N., & Kwok, O. (2007). Influence of student-teacher and parent-teacher relationships on low achieving readers' engagement and achievement in the primary grades. *Journal of Educational Psychology, 99*(1), 39–51.

Hughes, J. N., Luo, W., Kwok, O., & Loyd, L. L. (2008). Teacher-student support, effortful engagement, and achievement: A 3-year longitudinal study. *Journal of Educational Psychology, 100*(1), 1–14.

Jennings, G. (2003). An exploration of meaningful participation and caring relationships as contexts for school engagement. *California School Psychologist, 8,* 43–52.

Katz, M. (1997). *On playing a poor hand well.* New York: W.W. Norton.

King, J. and Lopez, D. (2008). *Turnaround schools.* TurnAround Schools.

Krovetz, M. L. (1999). Resiliency: Key element for supporting youth at-risk. *Clearing House, 73*(2), 1–5.

Kuykendall, C. (2004). *From rage to hope: Strategies for reclaiming Black & Hispanic students.* Bloomington, IL: National Educational Service.

Ladd, G. W., & Dinella, L. M. (2009). Continuity and change in early school engagement: Predictive of children's achievement trajectories from first to eighth grade? *Journal of Educational Psychology, 101*(1), 190–206.

Ladd, G. W., Birch, S. H., & Buhs, E. S. (1999). Children's social and scholastic lives in kindergarten: Related spheres of influence? *Child Development, 70,* 1373–1400.

Leithwood, K., & Jantzi, D. (2006). Transformational school leadership for large-scale reform: Effects on students, teachers, and their classroom practices. *School Effectiveness and School Improvement, 17*(2), 201–227.

Liew, J., Chen, Q., & Hughes, J. (2010). Child effortful control, teacher-student relationships, and achievement in academically at-risk children: Additive and interactive effects. *Early Childhood Research Quarterly, 25*(1), 51–64. doi: 10.1016/j.ecresq.2009.07.005.

Lumpkin, A. (2007). Caring teachers: The key to student learning. *Kappa Delta Pi Record, 43*(4), 158–160.

Lynn, M. (2006). Dancing between two worlds: A portrait of the life of a black male teacher in South Gentral LA. *International Journal of Qualitative Studies in Education. 19*(2), 221-242.

Martin, A., & Dowson, M. (2009). Interpersonal relationships, motivation, engagement, and achievement: Yields for theory, current issues, and educational practice. *Review of Educational Research, 79*(1), 327–365. Retrieved from Education Full Text database.

Mashburn, A. J., Pianta, R. C., Hamre, B. K., Downer, J. T., Barbarin, O. A., Bryant, D., et al. (2008). Measures of classroom quality in prekindergarten and children's development of academic, language, and social skills. *Child Development, 79,* 732–749.

McKinsey & Company. (2009). *The economic impact of the achievement gap in America's schools.* Retrieved from http://www.mckinsey.com/app_media/images/page_images/offices/socialsector/pdf/achievement_gap_report.pdf

Midcontinent Research for Education and Learning. (2010). *Changing the odds for student success: What matters most.* Retrieved from http://www.change theodds.org/

Morales, E. E. (2008). A focus on hope: Toward a more comprehensive theory of academic resiliency among at-risk minority students. *Journal of At-Risk Issues, 14*(1), 23–32.

Nelson, M. L., Tierney, S. S., Hau, J. M., & Englar-Garlson, M. E. (2006) Glass jumping into academia: Multiple identities for counseling academics. *Journal of Counseling Psychology. 53*, 1-14.

Neuman, S. (2009). *Changing the odds for children at risk: Seven essential principles of educational programs that break the cycle of poverty.* Westport, CT: Praeger.

Nevarez, C., & Wood, J. (2007). Developing urban school leaders: Building on solutions 15 years after the Los Angeles riots. *Educational Studies, 42*(3), 266–280. Retrieved from Education Full Text database.

Noam, G. G., & Fiore, N. (2004). Relationships across multiple settings: An overview. *New Directions for Youth Development, 103,* 9–16.

Noddings, N. (1988, December 7). Schools face crisis in caring. *Education Week.* p. 32

Noddings, N. 1992. The challenge to care in schools: *An alternative approach to education.* New York: Teachers College Press.

O'Connor, E., & McCartney, K. (2007). Examining teacher-child relationships and achievement as part of an ecological model of development. *American Educational Research Journal, 44*(2), 340–369.

Pianta, R., & Stuhlman, M. W. (2004). Teacher-child relationships and children's success in the first years of school. *School Psychology Review, 33*(3), 444–458.

Pianta, R., Belsky, J., Vandergrift, N., Houts, R., & Morrison, F. (2008). Classroom effects on children's achievement trajectories in elementary school. American *Educational Research Journal, 45*(2), 365–397. Retrieved from Education Full Text database.

Pitman, M.A., & Zorn, D. (2000). *Caring as tenacity: Stories of urban school survival.* Crosskill, NJ: Hampton Press.

Ponitz, C. C., Rimm-Kaufman, S. E., Grimm, K., & Curby, T. W. (2009). Kindergarten classroom quality, behavioral engagement, and reading achievement. *School Psychology Review, 38*(1), 102–120.

Rapp, D. (2002). Social justice and the importance of rebellious imaginations. *Journal of School Leadership, 12*(3), 226-245.

Riley, K. W. (2006). Resilient children in an imperfect world. *Leadership, 35*(4), 1–7.

Salinas, M., & Garr, J. (2009). Effect of learner-centered education on the academic outcomes of minority groups. *Journal of Instructional Psychology, 36*(3).

Scheurich, J. and Skrla, L. (2003). *Leadership for equity and excellence: Creating high achievement classrooms, schools, and districts.* Thousand Oaks, CA: Corwin.

Shepard, J. S. (2004). Multiple ways of knowing: Fostering resiliency though providing opportunities for participating in learning. *Reclaiming Children and Youth, 12*(4), 210–216.

Teven, J. J., & McCroskey, J. C. (1997). The relationship of perceived teacher caring with student learning and teacher evaluation. *Communication Education, 46,* 1–9.

Theoharis, G. (2007). Social justice educational leaders and resistance: Toward a theory of social justice leadership. *Educational Administration Quarterly, 43*(2), 221–258. doi: 10.1177/0013161X06293717

Thomas, V. G. (2000). Learner-centered alternatives to social promotion and retention: A talent development approach. *Journal of Negro Education, 69,* 323–337.

United States Census Bureau. (2009). *How the Census Bureau measures poverty.* Retrieved from http://www.census.gov/hhes/www/poverty/ about/ overview/measure .html

United States Department of Education. (2007). *High school dropout and completion rates in the United States: 2007.* Retrieved from http://www.dropoutprevention .org/stats/docs/high_school_dropout_and_copletion_rates_2007.pdf

United States Government Spending. (2011). *U.S. education spending.* Retrieved from http://www.usgovernmentspending.com/ us_education_ spending_20 .html#usgs30250

Wadsworth, M., & Santiago, C. (2008). Risk and resiliency processes in ethnically diverse families in poverty. *Journal of Family Psychology, 22*(3), 399–410. doi: 10.1037/0893-3200.22.3.399

Wehlage, G.G. and Rutter, R.A. (1986). Dropping out: How much do schools contribute to the problem? *Teachers College Record, 87,* 374-392.

Weinstein, R. S. (1991). Expectations and high school change: Teacher-researcher collaboration to prevent school failure. *American Journal of Community Psychology (19)*3.

Weinstein, R. S. (2002). Overcoming inequality in schooling: A call to action for community psychology. *American Journal of Community Psychology, 30,* 21–40.

Werner, E. and Smith, R. (2001). *Journeys from childhood to the midlife: Risk, resilience, and recovery.* New York: Cornell University Press.

WestEd. (2001). *Youth development strategies, concepts, and research.* Retrieved from http://www.wested.org/chks/pdf/rydm_supplement.pdf

WestEd. (2009). *California Healthy Kids Survey, 2007–2009, Statewide results: Main report.* Retrieved from http://chks.wested.org/resources/Elem_State_0709_ Main.pdf

Worthy, J., Patterson, E., Salas, R., Prater, S., & Turner, M. (2002). More than just reading: The human factor in reaching resistant readers. *Reading Research and Instruction, 41*(2), 177–202.

Index

Academic failure, 2
Academic turning points, 5
Accountability, 57
Achievement gap, 4 (figure), 4–5, 52
Ainley, J., 14
Alexander, K. L., 18
Anyon, J., 3
At-risk students, 2–8, 11–13, 42–48, 59
   see also Caring adult–student relationships;
      Kauai Study
Austin, G. A., 9, 14, 22–23 (table)

Banan, A., 75–77
Bandura, A., 11
Barbarin, O. A.
   see Mashburn, A. J.
Battistich, V., 14, 21
Becker, B. E., 2, 12
Behavior expectations, 75–77
Belsky, J., 17
Benard, B., 12, 15, 16, 17, 28, 28–29 (table), 32,
   33, 34, 37, 40, 41 (table)
Birch, S. H., 18
Bockern, S. V., 8
Bolman, L. G., 57
Brokenleg, M., 8
Bryant, D.
   see Mashburn, A. J.
Buhs, E. S., 18
Burns, T., 5

California, 4–5
California Healthy Kids Survey (CHKS), 7–9
California Standards Test (CST), 5
Canada, Geoffrey, 25
Caring adult–student relationships
   college readiness programs, 34–37, 61–63,
      65–67
   parent and family persistence, 32–34
   protective factors, 17–18, 19–20 (table)
   risk factors, 37–38

school rules, 37–38, 75–77
schoolwide support, 28, 28–29 (table)
social and emotional intelligences, 34
structural elements, 38
students' perspective, 25–38
student voice, 31–32
supportive persistence, 29–31, 30 (figure)
transformational leadership, 55–59
Carter, A., 75–77
Cecil, J., 75–77
Chen, Q., 19–20 (table)
Classroom goals, 79
College readiness programs, 36, 45–46,
   61–63, 65–67
Connectedness, 7–9
Connell, J. P., 14
Connor, C. M., 13
Cornelius-White, J., 18, 50
Courageous leadership, 56
Cuban, L., 8
Curby, T. W., 13
   see also Ponitz, C. C.

Darling–Hammond, L., 13
Deadly behaviors, 6–7
Deal, T. E., 57
Delpit, L., 8
Deming, W. E., 15
Deschenes, S., 8
Dinella, L. M., 22–23 (table)
Downer, J. T.
   see Mashburn, A. J.
Downey, J. A., 39–40
Dowson, M., 14
Dreamboards, 43–44, 44 (figure), 81
DuFour, Rebecca, 49
DuFour, Richard, 49

Eaker, R., 49
Earl, L., 14
Edmonds, R., 1

Educational funding, 3, 3 (figure)
Embry, D. D., 34, 38
Engaging classrooms
  college readiness programs, 45–46
  Dreamboards, 43–44, 44 (figure), 81
  hands-free accountability, 47–48
  implementation strategies, 42–48
  levels of support, 40, 41 (table), 89–92
  Reading Rocks, 44–45
  short-term goal setting, 42–43, 79
  student engagement, 39–40
  whiteboards, 46–47, 47 (figure)
Englar-Carson, M. E., 8
Enrichment opportunities, 69–70
Entwisle, D. R., 18
Escalante, Jaime, 58
Expectations, 5, 6 (table)

Federal spending, 2, 3 (figure)
Fiore, N., 18
Fisher, D., 87–88
Franco, B., 11
Frey, N., 87–88
Fullan, M., 57
Future of Children, 12

Gándara, P., 8
Garr, J., 50
Glanz, J., 56
Glende, J., 88
Goodenow, C., 14
Government spending, 2
Grade Improvement Plan, 31, 87–88
Greenwood, C. R., 22–23 (table)
Grimm, K., 13
  see also Ponitz, C. C.

Hall, Q., 11
Hall, Quantedius, 11
Hamre, B. K., 18, 19–20 (table)
  see also Mashburn, A. J.
Hands-free accountability, 47–48
Hanson, T. L., 9, 14, 22–23 (table)
Hargreaves, A., 14
Hattie, J. A. C., 18, 51, 83–84
Hau, J. M., 8
Hero/heroine short story project, 40
High-poverty schools, 3 (figure), 3–4, 12–13
Hindman, A. H.
  see Connor, C. M.
Hispanic achievement, 8
Hom, A., 14
Horton, B. T., 22–23 (table)
Houts, R., 17
Hughes, J. N., 12, 18, 19–20 (table),
  22–23 (table)

Jantzi, D., 55–56
Jennings, G., 21

Katz, M., 58–59
Kauai Study, 16–17
Keller, Helen, 58
King, J., 35
Krovetz, M. L., 5, 24
Kuykendall, C., 15, 85–86
Kwok, O., 12, 18, 19–20 (table), 22–23 (table)

Ladd, G. W., 18, 22–23 (table)
Leadership theory of social justice, 15–16
Learner- versus teacher-centered practices,
  50–52
Lee-Bayha, J., 14, 22–23 (table)
Leithwood, K., 55–56
Levels of support, 40, 41 (table), 89–92
Liew, J., 19–20 (table)
Life skills strategy, 67
Lopez, D., 35
Low expectations, 6–7
Loyd, L. L., 22–23 (table)
Lumpkin, A., 17, 58
Luo, W., 22–23 (table)
Luthar, S. S., 2, 12
Lynn, M., 8

Many, T., 49
Martin, A., 14
Mashburn, A. J., 13
McCartney, K., 19–20 (table)
McCroskey, J. C., 14
McKinsey & Company, 4
Meaningful student participation, 21,
  22–23 (table)
Mentor programs, 44–45
Meta Strategies for Student Growth (Hattie),
  83–84
Midcontinent Research for Education and
  Learning, 12, 17
Morales, E. E., 8, 15, 32
Moral purpose, 57
Morrison, F., 17
  see also Connor, C. M.
"My Plan for Success" growth plan,
  30 (figure), 31, 71–74, 85–86

Nelson, M. L., 8
Neuman, S., 12
Nevarez, C., 3
Noam, G. G., 18
Noddings, N., 17, 28
No Excuses network, 35

O'Connor, E., 19–20 (table)
"Own it" philosophy, 52–53, 56–57

Parent and family involvement, 32–34
Patterson, E., 19–20 (table)
Peer relationships, 37
Pianta, R. C., 14, 17, 18, 19–20 (table), 32
    see also Mashburn, A. J.
Pittman, M.A., 57
Plans for Success strategy, 43, 71–74, 85–86
Ponitz, C. C., 13, 14
Prater, S., 19–20 (table)

Rapp, D., 16
Reading achievement, 4, 4 (figure)
Reading Rocks, 44–45
Resiliency
    definition, 5
    Kauai Study, 16–17
    leadership theory of social justice, 15–16
    protective factors, 13–14, 17–26,
        19–20 (table), 22–23 (table), 59
    research studies, 7–13
    theoretical perspectives, 14–15
    transformational leadership, 55–59
    see also Caring adult–student relationships
Riley, K. W., 12, 38
Rimm-Kaufman, S. E., 13
    see also Ponitz, C. C.
Rutter, R. A., 18
Ryan, J., 14

Salas, R., 19–20 (table)
Salinas, M., 50
Santiago, C., 13
Scheurich, J., 16
School rules, 37–38, 75–77
"Schoolwide Game Plan, The" (Canada), 25
Sense of urgency, 52
Shepard, J. S., 5, 34
Short-term goal setting, 42–43, 79
Silent killers, 6–7
Skrla, L., 16
Smith, R., 16
Solomon, D., 21
Son, S.-H.
    see Connor, C. M.
Stanley, L., 19–20 (table)
Student-centered schools, 50–52
Student engagement, 21, 22–23 (table), 24,
        39–40
Student growth plan, 71–74
Student learning
    achievement gap, 52

cultural shifts, 49–50
    "own it" philosophy, 52–53, 56–57
    sense of urgency, 52
    teacher- versus learner-centered practices,
        50–52
    transformational leadership, 55–59
Stuhlman, M. W., 19–20 (table)
Sullivan, Anne, 58

Teacher- versus learner-centered practices,
        50–52
Tenacious caring, 57
Teven, J. J., 14
Theoharis, G., 15, 16, 55, 56
Thomas, V. G., 2
Tierney, S. S., 8
"Touch of the Master's Hand, The" (Welch),
        59–60
Transformational leadership
    change agents, 55–56
    ethical practices, 57
    "own it" philosophy, 56–57
Turner, M., 19–20 (table)
Turning points, 5, 59
Tyack, D., 8

Underfunded schools, 3
United States Census Bureau, 35, 36
United States Department of Education, 21
United States Government Spending, 2
Utley, C. A., 22–23 (table)

Vandergrift, N., 17
Vocabulary, college readiness,
        65–66

Wadsworth, M., 13
Watley, D., 42
Watson, M., 21
Wehlage, G. G., 18
Weinstein, R. S., 2
Welch, Myra B., 59–60
Wellborn, J. G., 14
Werner, E., 16
WestEd, 7, 9, 17
Whiteboards, 46–47, 47 (figure)
Winfrey, Oprah, 43
Wood, J., 3
Worthy, J., 19–20 (table)

Zorn, D., 57

CORWIN

A SAGE Company

The Corwin logo—a raven striding across an open book—represents the union of courage and learning. Corwin is committed to improving education for all learners by publishing books and other professional development resources for those serving the field of PreK–12 education. By providing practical, hands-on materials, Corwin continues to carry out the promise of its motto: **"Helping Educators Do Their Work Better."**